Sextus Empiricus and Greek Scepticism

Mary Mills Patrick

Contents

SEXTUS EMPIRICUS AND GREEK SCEPTICISM 7
PREFACE 8
CHAPTER I. 11
CHAPTER II. 33
CHAPTER III. 42
CHAPTER IV. 78
CHAPTER V. 96
BOOK I. 117
CHAPTER I. 117
CHAPTER II. 118
CHAPTER III. 119
CHAPTER IV. 119
CHAPTER V. 121
CHAPTER VI. 121
CHAPTER VII. 122
CHAPTER VIII. 123
CHAPTER IX. 124
CHAPTER X. 124
CHAPTER XI. 125
CHAPTER XII. 126
CHAPTER XIII. 128
CHAPTER XIV. 129
THE FIRST TROPE. 130
THE SECOND TROPE. 139
THE THIRD TROPE. 142
THE FOURTH TROPE. 144
THE FIFTH TROPE. 148
THE SIXTH TROPE. 150
THE SEVENTH TROPE. 151
THE EIGHTH TROPE. 152
THE NINTH TROPE. 154
THE TENTH TROPE. 155
CHAPTER XV. 159
CHAPTER XVI. 162
CHAPTER XVII. 163
CHAPTER XVIII. 165
CHAPTER XIX. 165
CHAPTER XX. 167
CHAPTER XXI. 167
CHAPTER XXII. 168
CHAPTER XXIII. 169
CHAPTER XXIV. 170
CHAPTER XXV. 171
CHAPTER XXVI. 171
CHAPTER XXVII. 172
CHAPTER XXVIII. 173
CHAPTER XXIX. 174
CHAPTER XXXI. 177
CHAPTER XXXII. 177
CHAPTER XXXIII. 179
CHAPTER XXXIV. 184

SEXTUS EMPIRICUS AND GREEK SCEPTICISM

BY

Mary Mills Patrick

SEXTUS EMPIRICUS
AND GREEK SCEPTICISM

A Thesis accepted for the Degree of Doctor of

Philosophy in the University of Bern

Switzerland, November 1897

by

MARY MILLS PATRICK PRESIDENT OF THE AMERICAN COLLEGE, CONSTANTINOPLE TURKEY

This Thesis is accompanied by a Translation from the Greek of the First Book of the "Pyrrhonic Sketches" by Sextus Empiricus

PREFACE

The following treatise on Sextus Empiricus and Greek Scepticism has been prepared to supply a need much felt in the English language by students of Greek philosophy. For while other schools of Greek philosophy have been exhaustively and critically discussed by English scholars, there are few sources of information available to the student who wishes to make himself familiar with the teachings of Pyrrhonism. The aim has been, accordingly, to give a concise presentation of Pyrrhonism in relation to its historical development and the Scepticism of the Academy, with critical references to the French and German works existing on the subject. The time and manner of the connection of Sextus Empiricus with the Pyrrhonean School has also been discussed.

As the First Book of the ***Hypotyposes***, or Pyrrhonic Sketches by Sextus Empiricus, contains the substance of the teachings of Pyrrhonism, it has been hoped that a translation of it into English might prove a useful contribution to the literature on Pyrrhonism, and this translation has been added to the critical part of the work.

In making this translation, and in the general study of the works of Sextus, the Greek text of Immanuel Bekker, Berlin, 1842, has been used, with frequent consultation of the text of J.A. Fabricius, 1718, which was taken directly from the existing manuscripts of the works of Sextus. The divisions into chapters, with the headings of the chapters in the translation, is the same as Fabricius gives from the manuscripts, although not used by Bekker, and the numbers of the paragraphs are the same as those given by both Fabricius and Bekker. References to Diogenes Laertius and other ancient works have been carefully verified.

The principal modern authors consulted are the following:

Ritter, **Geschichte der Philosophie**, II. Auf., Hamburg, 1836-38.

Zeller, **Philosophie der Griechen**, III. Auf., Leipzig, 1879-89.

Lewes, **History of Philosophy**, Vol. I., London, 1866.

Ueberweg, **History of Philosophy**, IV. ed., translated by Morris, 1871.

Brochard, **Les Sceptiques Grecs**, Paris, 1877.

Brochard, **Pyrrhon et le Scepticism Primitive**, No. 5, Ribot's **Revue Phil.**, Paris, 1885.

Saisset, **Le Scepticism Aenesideme-Pascal-Kant**, Paris, 1867.

Chaignet, **Histoire de la Psychologie des Grecs**, Paris, 1887-90.

Haas, **Leben des Sextus Empiricus**, Burghausen, 1882.

Natorp, Forschungen zur Geschichte des Erkenntnisproblems bei den Alten, Berlin, 1884.

Hirzel, *Untersuchungen zu Cicero's philosophischen Schriften*, Leipzig, 1877-83.

Pappenheim, Erlaeuterung zu des Sextus Empiricus Pyrrhoneischen Grundzuegen, Heidelberg, 1882.

Pappenheim, *Die Tropen der Greichischen Skeptiker*, Berlin, 1885.

Pappenheim, *Lebensverhaeltnisse des Sextus Empiricus*, Berlin, 1887.

Pappenheim, Der angebliche Heraclitismus des Skeptikers Ainesidemos, Berlin, 1887.

Pappenheim, Der Sitz der Schule der Griechischen Skeptiker, Archiv fuer Geschichte der Philosophie, I. 1, S. 47, 1887.

Maccoll, *The Greek Sceptics from Pyrrho to Sextus*, London, 1869.

My grateful acknowledgments are due to Dr. Ludwig Stein, Professor of Philosophy in the University of Bern, for valuable assistance in relation to the plan of the work and advice in regard to the best authorities to be consulted. Thanks are also due to Dr. Louisos Iliou, of Robert College, Constantinople, for kind suggestions concerning the translation.

CHAPTER I.

The Historical Relations of Sextus Empiricus.

Interest has revived in the works of Sextus Empiricus in recent times, especially, one may say, since the date of Herbart. There is much in the writings of Sextus that finds a parallel in the methods of modern philosophy. There is a common starting-point in the study of the power and limitations of human thought. There is a common desire to investigate the phenomena of sense-perception, and the genetic relations of man to the lower animals, and a common interest in the theory of human knowledge.

While, however, some of the pages of Sextus' works would form a possible introduction to certain lines of modern philosophical thought, we cannot carry the analogy farther, for Pyrrhonism as a whole lacked the essential element of all philosophical progress, which is a belief in the possibility of finding and establishing the truth in the subjects investigated.

Before beginning a critical study of the writings of Sextus Empiricus, and the light which they throw on the development of Greek Scepticism, it is necessary to make ourselves somewhat familiar with the environment in which he lived and wrote. We shall thus be able to comprehend more fully the standpoint from which he regarded philosophical questions.

Let us accordingly attempt to give some details of his life, including his profession, the time when he lived, the place of his birth, the country in which he taught, and the general aim and character of his works. Here, however, we encounter great difficulties, for although we possess most of the writings of Sextus well preserved, the evidence which they provide on the points mentioned is very slight. He does not give us biographical details in regard to himself, nor does he refer to his contemporaries in a way to afford any exact knowledge of them. His name even furnishes us with a problem impossible of solution. He is called [Greek: Sextos ho empeirikos] by Diogenes Laertius[1]: [Greek: Herodotou de diekouse Sextos ho empeirikos hou kai ta deka ton skeptikon kai alla kallista' Sextou de diekouse Satorninos ho Kythenas, empeirikos kai autos]. Although in this passage Diogenes speaks of Sextus the second time without the surname, we cannot understand the meaning otherwise than that Diogenes considered Sextus a physician of the Empirical School. Other evidence also is not wanting that Sextus bore this surname. Fabricius, in his edition of the works of Sextus, quotes from the *Tabella de Sectis Medicorum* of Lambecius the statement that Sextus was called Empiricus because of his position in medicine.[2]

Pseudo-Galen also refers to him as one of the directors of the Empirical School, and calls him [Greek: Sextos ho empeirikos].[3] His name is often found in the manuscripts written with the surname, as for example at the end of Logic II.[4] In other places it is found written without the surname, as Fabricius testifies, where Sextus is mentioned as a Sceptic in connection with Pyrrho.

[1] Diog. Laert. IX. 12, 116.

[2] Fabricius *Testimonia*, p. 2.

[3] Pseudo-Galen *Isag.* 4; Fabricius *Testimonia*, p. 2.

[4] Bekker *Math.* VIII. 481.

The Sceptical School was long closely connected with the Empirical School of medicine, and the later Pyrrhoneans, when they were physicians, as was often the case, belonged for the most part to this school. Menedotus of Nicomedia is the first Sceptic, however, who is formally spoken of as an Empirical physician,[1] and his contemporary Theodas of Laodicea was also an Empirical physician. The date of Menedotus and Theodas is difficult to fix, but Brochard and Hass agree that it was about 150 A.D.[2] After the time of these two physicians, who were also each in turn at the head of the Sceptical School,[3] there seems to have been a definite alliance between Pyrrhonism and Empiricism in medicine, and we have every reason to believe that this alliance existed until the time of Sextus.

[1] Diog. IX. 12, 115.

[2] Brochard *Op. cit. Livre* IV. p. 311.

[3] Diog. IX. 12, 116.

The difficulty in regard to the name arises from Sextus' own testimony. In the first book of the *Hypotyposes* he takes strong ground against the identity of Pyrrhonism and Empiricism in medicine. Although he introduces his objections with the admission that "some say that they are the same," in recognition of the close union that had existed between them, he goes on to say that "Empiricism is neither Scepticism itself, nor would it suit the Sceptic to take that sect upon himself",[1] for the reason that Empiricism maintains dogmatically the impossibility of knowledge, but he would prefer to belong to the Methodical School, which was the only medical school worthy of the Sceptic. "For this alone of all the medical sects, does not proceed rashly it seems to me, in regard to unknown things, and does not presume to say whether they are comprehensible or not, but it is guided by phenomena.[2] It will thus be seen that the Methodical School of medicine has a certain relationship to Scepticism which is closer than that of the other medical sects."[3]

[1] *Hyp*. I. 236.

[2] *Hyp*. I. 237.

[3] *Hyp*. I. 241.

We know from the testimony of Sextus himself that he was a physician. In one case he uses the first person for himself as a physician,[1] and in another he speaks of Asclepius as "the founder of our science,"[2] and all his illustrations show a breadth and variety of medical knowledge that only a physician could possess. He published a medical work which he refers to once as [Greek: iatrika hupomnemata],[3] and again as [Greek: empeirika hupomnemata][4] These passages probably refer to the same work,[5] which, unfortunately for the solution of the difficult question that we have in hand, is lost, and nothing is known of its contents.

In apparent contradiction to his statement in *Hypotyposes* I., that Scepticism and Empiricism are opposed to each other, in that Empiricism denies the possibility of knowledge, and Scepticism makes no dogmatic statements of any kind, Sextus classes the Sceptics and Empiricists together in another instance, as regarding knowledge as impossible[6] [Greek: all oi men phasin auta me katalambanesthai, hoster hoi apo tes empeirias iatroi kai hoi apo tes skepseos phiolosophoi]. In another case, on the contrary, he contrasts the Sceptics sharply with the Empiricists in regard to the [Greek: apodeixeis].[7] [Greek: hoi de empeirikoi anairousin, hoi de skeptikoi en epoche tauten ephylaxan].

[1] *Hyp*. ii. 238.

[2] *Adv. Math*. A. 260.

[3] *Adv. Math*. vii. 202.

[4] *Adv. Math*. A. 61.

[5] Zeller *Op. cit.*. iii. 43.

[6] *Adv. Math.* viii. 191.

[7] *Adv. Math.* VIII. 328.

Pappenheim thinks that Sextus belonged to the Methodical School, both from his strong expression in favor of that school in *Hyp*. I. 236, as above, and also because many of his medical opinions, as found in his works, agree with the teachings of the Methodical School, more nearly than with those of the Empiricists. Pappenheim also claims that we find no inconsistency with this view in the passage given where Sextus classes the Sceptics with the Empiricists, but considers that statement an instance of carelessness in expressing himself, on the part of Sextus.[1]

[1] *Lebensverhaeltnisse des Sex. Em.* 36.

The position of Pappenheim is assailable for the reason that in dealing with any problem regarding an author on the basis of internal evidence, we have no right to consider one of his statements worthy of weight, and another one unworthy, on the supposition that he expressed himself carelessly in the second instance. Rather must we attempt to find his true standpoint by fairly meeting all the difficulties offered in apparently conflicting passages. This has been attempted by Zeller, Brochard, Natorp and others, with the general result that all things considered they think without doubt that Sextus belonged to the Empirical School.[1] His other references are too strong to allow his fidelity to it to be doubted. He is called one of the leaders of Empiricism by Pseudo-Galen, and his only medical work bore the title [Greek: empeirika hupomnemata.] The opinion of the writers above referred to is that the passage which we have quoted from the *Hypotyposes* does not necessarily mean that Sextus was not an Empiricist, but as he was more of a Sceptic than a physician, he gave preference to those doctrines that were most consistent with Scepticism, and accordingly claimed that it was not absolutely necessary that a Sceptic physician should be an Empiricist. Natorp considers that the different standpoint from which Sextus judges the Empirical and Methodical Schools in his different works is accounted for on the supposition that he was an Empiricist, but disagreed with that school on the one point only.[2] Natorp points out that Sextus does not speak more favourably of the medical stand of the Methodical School, but only compares the way in which both schools regarded the question of the possibility of knowledge, and thinks that Sextus could have been an Empiricist as a physician notwithstanding his condemnation of the attitude of the Empirical School in relation to the theory of knowledge. This difference between the two schools was a small one, and on a subtle and unimportant point; in fact, a difference in philosophical theory, and not in medical practice.

[1] Brochard *Op. cit. Livre* IV. 317; Zeller *Op. cit.* III. 15; Natorp *Op. cit.* p. 155.

[2] Natorp *Op. cit*. 157.

While we would agree with the authors above referred to, that Sextus very probably recognized the bond between the Empirical School of medicine and Pyrrhonism, yet to make his possible connection with that school the explanation of his name, gives him more prominence as a physician than is consistent with what we know of his career. The long continued union of Empiricism and Scepticism would naturally support the view that Sextus was, at least during the earlier part of his life, a physician of that school, and yet it may be that he was not named Empiricus for that reason. There is one instance in ancient writings where Empiricus is known as a simple proper name.[1] It may have been a proper name in Sextus' case, or there are many other ways in which it could have originated, as those who have studied the origin of names will readily grant, perhaps indeed, from the title of the above-named work, [Greek: empeirika hupomnemata.] The chief argument for this view of the case is that there were other leaders of the Sceptical School, for whom we can claim far greater influence as Empiricists than for Sextus, and for whom the surname Empiricus would have been more appropriate, if it was given in consequence of prominence in the Empirical School. Sextus is known to the world as a Sceptic, and not as a physician. He was classed in later times with Pyrrho, and his philosophical works survived, while his medical writings did not, but are chiefly known from his own mention of them. Moreover, the passage which we have quoted from the ***Hypotyposes*** is too strong to allow us easily to believe that Sextus remained all his life a member of the Empirical School. He could hardly have said, "Nor would it suit the Sceptic to take that sect upon himself," if he at the same time belonged to it. His other references to the Empirical School, of a more favorable character, can be easily explained on the ground of the long continued connection which had existed between the two schools. It is quite possible to suppose that Sextus was an Empiricist a part of his life, and afterwards found the Methodical School more to his liking, and such a change would not in any way have affected his stand as a physician.

[1] Pappenheim ***Leb. Ver. Sex. Em***. 6.

In regard to the exact time when Sextus Empiricus lived, we gain very little knowledge from internal evidence, and outside sources of information are equally uncertain. Diogenes Laertius must have been a generation younger than Sextus, as he mentions the disciple of Sextus, Saturninus, as an Empirical physician.[1] The time of Diogenes is usually estimated as the first half of the third century A.D.,[2] therefore Sextus cannot be brought forward later than the beginning of the century. Sextus, however, directs his writings entirely against the Dogmatics, by whom he distinctly states that he means the Stoics,[3] and the influence of the Stoics began to decline in the beginning of the third century A.D. A fact often used as a help in fixing the date of Sextus is his mention of Basilides the Stoic,[4] [Greek: alla kai oi stoikoi, os oi peri ton Basileiden]. This Basilides was supposed to be identical with one of the teachers of Marcus Aurelius.[5] This is accepted by Zeller in the second edition of his ***History of Philosophy***, but not in the third for the reason that Sextus, in all the work from which this reference is taken, *i.e. Math*. VII.-XI., mentions no one besides Aenesidemus, who lived later than the middle of the last century B.C.[6] The Basilides referred to by Sextus may be one mentioned in a list of twenty Stoics, in a fragment of Diogenes Laertius, recently published in Berlin by Val Rose.[7] Too much importance has, however, been given to the relation of the mention of Basilides the Stoic to the question of the date of Sextus. Even if the Basilides referred to by Sextus is granted to have been the teacher of Marcus Aurelius, it only serves to show that Sextus lived either at the same time with Marcus Aurelius or after him, which is a conclusion that we must in any case reach for other reasons.

[1] Diog. IX. 12, 116.

[2] Ueberweg *Hist. of Phil.* p. 21.

[3] Hyp. I. 65.

[4] *Adv. Math*. VII. 258.

[5] Fabricius *Vita Sexti.*

[6] Zeller *Op. cit*. III. 8.

[7] Brochard *Op. cit*. IV. 315.

The fact that has caused the greatest uncertainty in regard to the date of Sextus is that Claudius Galen in his works mentions several Sceptics who were also physicians of the Empirical School,[1] and often speaks of Herodotus, supposed to be identical with the teacher of Sextus given by Diogenes

Laertius,[2] but makes no reference whatever to Sextus. As Galen's time passes the limit of the second century A.D., we must either infer that Sextus was not the well-known physician that he was stated to be by Pseudo-Galen, and consequently not known to Galen, or that Galen wrote before Sextus became prominent as a Sceptic. This silence on the part of Galen in regard to Sextus increases the doubt, caused by Sextus' own criticism of the Empirical School of medicine, as to his having been an Empiricist. The question is made more complicated, as it is difficult to fix the identity of the Herodotus so often referred to by Galen.[3] As Galen died about 200 A.D. at the age of seventy,[4] we should fix the date of Sextus early in the third century, and that of Diogenes perhaps a little later than the middle, were it not that early in the third century the Stoics began to decline in influence, and could hardly have excited the warmth of animosity displayed by Sextus. We must then suppose that Sextus wrote at the very latter part of the second century, and either that Galen did not know him, or that Galen's books were published before Sextus became prominent either as a physician or as a Sceptic. The fact that he may have been better known as the latter than as the former does not sufficiently account for Galen's silence, as other Sceptics are mentioned by him of less importance than Sextus, and the latter, even if not as great a physician as Pseudo-Galen asserts, was certainly both a Sceptic and a physician, and must have belonged to one of the two medical schools so thoroughly discussed by Galen--either the Empirical or the Methodical. Therefore, if Sextus were a contemporary of Galen, he was so far removed from the circle of Galen's acquaintances as to have made no impression upon him, either as a Sceptic or a physician, a supposition that is very improbable. We must then fix the date of Sextus late in the second century, and conclude that the climax of his public career was reached after Galen had finished those of his writings which are still extant.

[1] Zeller, III. 7.

[2] Diog. XI. 12, 116.

[3] Pappenheim *Lebens. Ver. Sex. Em.* 30.

[4] Zeller *Grundriss der Ges. der Phil.* p. 260.

Sextus has a Latin name, but he was a Greek; we know this from his own statement.[1] We also know that he must have been a Greek from the beauty and facility of his style, and from his acquaintance with Greek dialects. The place of his birth can only, however, be conjectured, from arguments indirectly derived from his writings. His constant references throughout his works to the minute customs of different nations ought to give us a clue to the solution of this question, but strange to say they do not give us a decided one. Of these references a large number, however, relate to the customs of Libya, showing a minute knowledge in regard to the political and religious customs of this land that he displays in regard to no other country except Egypt.[2] Fabricius thinks Libya was not his birth place because of a reference which he makes to it in the *Hypotyposes*--[Greek: Thrakon de kai Gaitoulon (Libyon de ethnos touto)].[3] This conclusion is, however, entirely unfounded, as the explanation of Sextus simply shows that the people whom he was then addressing were not familiar with the nations of Libya. Suidas speaks of two men called Sextus, one from Chaeronea and one from Libya, both of whom he calls Sceptics, and to one of whom he attributes Sextus' books. All authorities agree in asserting that great confusion exists in the works of Suidas; and Fabricius, Zeller, and Pappenheim place no weight upon this testimony of Suidas.[4] Haas, however, contends[5] that it is unreasonable to suppose that this confusion could go as far as to attribute the writings of Sextus Empiricus to Sextus of Chaeronea, and also make the latter a Sceptic, and he considers it far more reasonable to accept the testimony of Suidas, as it coincides so well with the internal evidence of Sextus' writings in regard to his native land. It is nevertheless evident, from his familiarity with the customs, language, and laws of Athens, Alexandria and Rome, that he must have resided at some time in each of these cities.

[1] *Adv. Math.* A. 246; *Hyp.* I. 152; *Hyp.* III. 211, 214.

[2] Haas *Op. cit.* p. 10.

[3] *Hyp.* III. 213.

[4] Pappenheim *Lebens. Ver. Sex. Em.* 5, 22; Zeller Op. cit. *III. 39; Fabricius* Vita de Sextus.

[5] Haas *Op. cit.* p. 6.

Of all the problems connected with the historical details of the life of Sextus, the one that is the most difficult of solution, and also the most important for our present purpose of making a critical study of his teaching, is to fix the seat of the Sceptical School during the time that he was in charge of it. The *Hypotyposes* are lectures delivered in public in that period of his life. Where then were they delivered? We know that the Sceptical School must have had a long continued existence as a definite philosophical movement, although some have contended otherwise. The fact of its existence as an organized direction of thought, is demonstrated by its formulated teachings, and the list given by Diogenes Laertius of its principal leaders,[1] and by references from the writings of Sextus. In the first book of *Hypotyposes* he refers to Scepticism as a distinct system of philosophy, [Greek: kai taen diakrisin taes skepseos apo ton parakeimenon autae philosophion].[2] He speaks also of the older Sceptics,[3] and the later Sceptics.[4]

Pyrrho, the founder of the school, taught in Elis, his native village; but even as early as the time of Timon, his immediate follower, his teachings were somewhat known in Alexandria, where Timon for a while resided.[5] The immediate disciples of Timon, as given by Diogenes, were not men known in Greece or mentioned in Greek writings. Then we have the well-known testimony of Aristocles the Peripatetic in regard to Aenesidemus, that he taught Pyrrhonism in Alexandria[6]--[Greek: echthes kai proaen en Alexandreia tae kat' Aigypton Ainaesidaemos tis anazopyrein aerxato ton huthlon touton].

[1] Diog. XI. 12, 115, 116.

[2] *Hyp*. I. 5.

[3] *Hyp*. I. 36.

[4] *Hyp*. I. 164.

[5] Chaignet *Op. cit*. 45.

[6] Aristocles of Euseb. *Praep. Ev.* XIV. E. 446.

This was after the dogmatic tendency of the Academy under Antiochus and his followers had driven Pyrrhonism from the partial union with the Academy, which it had experienced after the breaking up of the school under the immediate successors of Timon. Aenesidemus taught about the time of our era in Alexandria, and established the school there anew; and his followers are spoken of in a way that presupposes their continuing in the same place. There is every reason to think that the connection of Sextus with Alexandria was an intimate one, not only because Alexandria had been for so long a time the seat of Pyrrhonism, but also from internal evidence from his writings and their subsequent historical influence; and yet the ***Hypotyposes*** could not have been delivered in Alexandria, as he often refers to that place in comparison with the place where he was then speaking. He says, furthermore, that he teaches in the same place where his master taught.[1] [Greek: Blepon te hoti entha ho huphaegaetaes ho emos dielegeto, entautha ego nun dialegomai]. Therefore the school must have been removed from Alexandria, in or before the time of the teacher of Sextus, to some other centre. The ***Hypotyposes*** are from beginning to end a direct attack on the Dogmatics; therefore Sextus must have taught either in some city where the dogmatic philosophy was strong, or in some rival philosophical centre. The ***Hypotyposes*** show also that the writer had access to some large library. Alexandria, Rome and Athens are the three places the most probable for selection for such a purpose. For whatever reason the seat of the school was removed from Alexandria by the master of Sextus, or by himself, from the place where it had so long been united with the Empirical School of medicine, Athens would seem the most suitable city for its recontinuance, in the land where Pyrrhonism first had its birth. Sextus, however, in one instance, in referring to things invisible because of their outward relations, says in illustration, "as the city of Athens is invisible to us at present."[2] In other places also he contrasts the Athenians with the people whom he is addressing, equally with the Alexandrians, thus putting Athens as well as Alexandria out of the question.

[1] *Hyp.* III. 120.

[2] *Hyp.* II. 98.

Of the different writers on Sextus Empiricus, those who have treated this part of the subject most critically are Haas and Pappenheim. We will therefore consider, somewhat at length, the results presented by these two authors. Haas thinks that the *Hypotyposes* were delivered in Rome for the following reasons. Sextus' lectures must have been given in some centre of philosophical schools and of learning. He never opposes Roman relations to those of the place where he is speaking, as he does in regard to Athens and Alexandria. He uses the name "Romans" only three times,[1] once comparing them to the Rhodians, once to the Persians, and once in general to other nations.[2] In the first two of these references, the expression "among the Romans" in the first part of the antithesis is followed by the expression, "among us," in the second part, which Haas understands to be synonymous. The third reference is in regard to a Roman law, and the use of the word 'Roman' does not at all show that Sextus was not then in Rome. The character of the laws referred to by Sextus as [Greek: par' haemin] shows that they were always Roman laws, and his definition of law[3] is especially a definition of Roman law. This argument might, it would seem, apply to any part of the Roman Empire, but Haas claims that the whole relation of law to custom as treated of by Sextus, and all his statements of customs forbidden at that time by law, point to Rome as the place of his residence. Further, Haas considers the Herodotus mentioned by Galen[4] as a prominent physician in Rome, to have been the predecessor and master of Sextus, in whose place Sextus says that he is teaching.[5] Haas also thinks that Sextus' refutation of the identity of Pyrrhonism with Empiricism evidently refers to a paragraph in Galen's *Subfiguratio Empirica*,[6] which would be natural if the *Hypotyposes* were written shortly after Galen's *Sub. Em.*, and in the same place. Further, Hippolytus, who wrote in or near Rome very soon after the time of Sextus, apparently used the *Hypotyposes*, which would be more natural if he wrote in the same place. According to Haas, every thing in internal evidence, and outward testimony, points to Rome as having been the city where Sextus occupied his position as the head of the Sceptical School.

[1] Haas *Op. cit.* p. 15.

[2] *Hyp.* I. 149, 152; III. 211.

[3] *Hyp.* I. 146.

[4] Galen *de puls.* IV. 11; Bd. VIII. 751.

[5] *Hyp*. III. 120.

[6] Galen *Sub. Em.* 123 B-126 D. (Basileae, 1542).

Coming now to the position of Pappenheim on this subject, we find that he takes very decided ground against the seat of the Sceptical School having been in Rome, even for a short time, in his latest publication regarding it.[1] This opinion is the result of late study on the part of Pappenheim, for in his work on the *Lebensverhaeltnisse des Sextus Empiricus* Berlin 1875, he says, "Dass Herodotus in Rom lebte sagt Galen. Vermuthlich auch

Sextus." His reasons given in the later article for not connecting the Sceptical School at all with Rome are as follows. He finds no proof of the influence of Scepticism in Rome, as Cicero remarks that Pyrrhonism is extinct,[2] and he also gives weight to the well-known sarcastic saying of Seneca, Quis est qui tradat praecepta Pyrrhonis![3] While Haas claims that Sextus would naturally seek one of the centres of dogmatism, in order most effectively to combat it, Pappenheim, on the contrary, contends that it would have been foolishness on the part of Sextus to think of starting the Sceptical School in Rome, where Stoicism was the favored philosophy of the Roman Emperors; and when either for the possible reason of strife between the Empirical and Methodical Schools, or for some other cause, the Pyrrhonean School was removed from Alexandria, Pappenheim claims that all testimony points to the conclusion that it was founded in some city of the East. The name of Sextus is never known in Roman literature, but in the East, on the contrary, literature speaks for centuries of Sextus and Pyrrho. The *Hypotyposes*, especially, were well-known in the East, and references to Sextus are found there in philosophical and religious dogmatic writings. The Emperor Julian makes use of the works of Sextus, and he is frequently quoted by the Church Fathers of the Eastern Church.[4] Pappenheim accordingly concludes that the seat of Pyrrhonism after the school was removed from Alexandria, was in some unknown city of the East.

[1] Pappenheim Sitz der Skeptischen Schule. Archiv fuer Geschichte der Phil. 1888.

[2] Cicero *De Orat.* III. 17, 62.

[3] Seneca *nat. qu.* VII. 32. 2.

[4] Fabricius *de Sexto Empirico Testimonia*.

In estimating the weight of these arguments, we must accept with Pappenheim the close connection of Pyrrhonism with Alexandria, and the subsequent influence which it exerted upon the literature of the East. All historical relations tend to fix the permanent seat of Pyrrhonism, after its separation from the Academy, in Alexandria. There is nothing to point to its removal from Alexandria before the time of Menodotus, who is the teacher of Herodotus,[1] and for many reasons to be considered the real teacher of Sextus. It was Menodotus who perfected the Empirical doctrines, and who brought about an official union between Scepticism and Empiricism, and who gave Pyrrhonism in great measure, the *eclat* that it enjoyed in Alexandria, and who appears to have been the most powerful influence in the school, from the time of Aenesidemus to that of Sextus. Furthermore, Sextus' familiarity with Alexandrian customs bears the imprint of original knowledge, and he cannot, as Zeller implies, be accepted as simply quoting. One could hardly agree with Zeller,[2] that the familiarity shown by Sextus with the customs of both Alexandria and Rome in the *Hypotyposes* does not necessarily show that he ever lived in either of those places, because a large part of his works are compilations from other books; but on the contrary, the careful reader of Sextus' works must find in all of them much evidence of personal knowledge of Alexandria, Athens and Rome.

[1] Diog. IX. 12, 116.

[2] Zeller *Op. cit.* III. p. 39.

A part of Sextus' books also may have been written in Alexandria. [Greek: Pros phusikous] could have been written in

Alexandria.[1] If these were also lectures, then Sextus taught in Alexandria as well as elsewhere. The history of Eastern literature for the centuries immediately following the time of Sextus, showing as it does in so many instances the influence of Pyrrhonism, and a knowledge of the *Hypotyposes*, furnishes us with an incontestable proof that the school could not have been for a long time removed from the East, and the absence of such knowledge in Roman literature is also a strong argument against its long continuance in that city. It would seem, however, from all the data at command, that during the years that the Sceptical School was removed from Alexandria, its head quarters were in Rome, and that the Pyrrhonean *Hypotyposes* were delivered in Rome. Let us briefly consider the arguments in favour of such a hypothesis. Scepticism was not unknown in Rome. Pappenheim quotes the remark of Cicero that Pyrrhonism was long since dead, and the sarcasm of Seneca, Quis est qui tradat praecepta Pyrrhonis? as an argument against the knowledge of Pyrrhonism in Rome. We must remember, however, that in Cicero's time Aenesidemus had not yet separated himself from the Academy; or if we consider the Lucius Tubero to whom Aenesidemus dedicated his works, as the same Lucius Tubero who was the friend of Cicero in his youth, and accordingly fix the date of Aenesidemus about 50 B.C.,[2] even then Aenesidemus' work in Alexandria was too late to have necessarily been known to Cicero, whose remark must have been referred to the old school of Scepticism. Should we grant, however, that the statements of Cicero and Seneca prove that in their time Pyrrhonism was extinct in Rome, they certainly do not show that after their death it could not have again revived, for the *Hypotyposes* were delivered more than a century after the death of Seneca. There are very few writers in Aenesidemus' own time who showed any influence of his teachings.[3] This influence was felt later, as Pyrrhonism became better known. That Pyrrhonism received some attention in Rome before the time of Sextus is nevertheless demonstrated by the teachings of Favorinus there. Although Favorinus was known as an Academician, the title of his principal work was [Greek: tous philosophoumenous auto ton logon, hon aristoi hoi Purrhoneioi].[4] Suidas calls Favorinus a great author and learned in all science and philosophy,[5] and Favorinus made Rome the centre of his teaching and writing. His date is fixed by Zeller at 80-150 A.D., therefore Pyrrhonism was known in Rome shortly before the time of Sextus.

[1] Pappenheim Sitz der Skeptischen Schule; Archiv fuer Geschichte der Phil., *1888;* Adv. Math. X. 15, 95.

[2] Zeller *Op. cit.* III. 10.

[3] Zeller *Op. cit.* p. 63.

[4] Zeller *Op. cit.* p. 67.

[5] Brochard *Op. cit.* 329.

The whole tone of the *Hypotyposes*, with the constant references to the Stoics as living present opponents, shows that these lectures must have been delivered in one of the centres of Stoicism. As Alexandria and Athens are out of the question, all testimony points to Rome as having been the seat of the Pyrrhonean School, for at least a part of the time that Sextus was at its head. We would then accept the teacher of Sextus, in whose place he says he taught, as the Herodotus so often referred to by Galen[1] who lived in Rome. Sextus' frequent references to Asclepiades, whom he mentions ten different times by name in his works,[2] speak in favour of Rome in the matter under discussion, as Asclepiades made that city one of the

centres of medical culture. On the other hand, the fact that
there is no trace of the *Hypotyposes* in later Roman
literature, with the one exception of the works of Hippolytus,
as opposed to the wide-spread knowledge of them shown in the
East for centuries, is incontestable historical proof that the
Sceptical School could not long have had its seat at Rome. From
the two passages given above from Sextus' work against physics,
he must either have written that book in Alexandria, it would
seem, or have quoted those passages from some other work. May we
not then conclude, that Sextus was at the head of the school in
Rome for a short time, where it may have been removed
temporarily, on account of the difficulty with the Empiricists,
implied in *Hyp*. I. 236-241, or in order to be better able to
attack the Stoics, but that he also taught in Alexandria, where
the real home of the school was certainly found? There it
probably came to an end about fifty years after the time of
Sextus, and from that centre the Sceptical works of Sextus had
their wide-spread influence in the East.

[1] Galen VIII. 751.

[2] Bekker *Index*.

The books of Sextus Empiricus furnish us with the best and
fullest presentation of ancient Scepticism which has been
preserved to modern times, and give Sextus the position of one
of the greatest men of the Sceptical School. His works which are
still extant are the *Pyrrhonean Hypotyposes* in three volumes,
and the two works comprising eleven books which have been united
in later times under the title of [Greek: pros mathematikous],
one of which is directed against the sciences in general, and
the other against the dogmatic philosophers. The six books
composing the first of these are written respectively against

grammarians, rhetoricians, geometricians, arithmeticians, astronomers and musicians. The five books of the latter consist of two against the logicians, two against physics, and one against systems of morals. If the last short work of the first book directed against the arithmeticians is combined with the one preceding against the geometricians, as it well could be, the two works together would be divided into ten different parts; there is evidence to show that in ancient times such a division was made.[1] There were two other works of Sextus which are now lost, the medical work before referred to, and a book entitled [Greek: peri psuches]. The character of the extant works of Sextus is similar, as they are all directed either against science or against the dogmatics, and they all present the negative side of Pyrrhonism. The vast array of arguments comprising the subject-matter, often repeated in the same and different forms, are evidently taken largely from the Sceptical works which Sextus had resource to, and are, in fact, a summing up of all the wisdom of the Sceptical School. The style of these books is fluent, and the Greek reminds one of Plutarch and Thucydides, and although Sextus does not claim originality, but presents in all cases the arguments of the Sceptic, yet the illustrations and the form in which the arguments are presented, often bear the marks of his own thought, and are characterized here and there by a wealth of humor that has not been sufficiently noticed in the critical works on Sextus. Of all the authors who have reviewed Sextus, Brochard is the only one who seems to have understood and appreciated his humorous side.

We shall now proceed to the consideration of the general position and aim of Pyrrhonism.

[1] Diog. IX. 12, 116.

CHAPTER II.

The Position and Aim of Pyrrhonism.

The first volume of the ***Pyrrhonean Hypotyposes*** gives the most complete statement found in any of the works of Sextus Empiricus of the teachings of Pyrrhonism and its relation to other schools of philosophy. The chief source of the subject-matter presented is a work of the same name by Aenesidemus,[1] either directly used by Sextus, or through the writings of those who followed Aenesidemus. The comprehensive title [Greek: Purrhoneioi hupotuposeis] was very probably used in general to designate courses of lectures given by the leaders of the Sceptical School.

In the opening chapters of the ***Hypotyposes*** Sextus undertakes to define the position and aim of Pyrrhonism.[2] In introducing his subject he treats briefly of the differences between philosophical schools, dividing them into three classes; those which claim that they have found the truth, like the schools of Aristotle and Epicurus and the Stoics; those which deny the possibility of finding it, like that of the Academicians; and those that still seek it, like the Sceptical School. The accusation against the Academicians, that they denied the possibility of finding the truth, was one that the Sceptics were very fond of making. We shall discuss the justice of it later, simply remarking here, that to affirm the "incomprehensibility of the unknown," was a form of expression that the Pyrrhonists themselves were sometimes betrayed into, notwithstanding their careful avoidance of dogmatic statements.[3]

[1] Diog. IX. 11, 78.

[2] *Hyp.* I. 3, 4.

[3] *Adv. Math.* VIII. 191.

After defining the three kinds of philosophy as the Dogmatic, the Academic and the Sceptic, Sextus reminds his hearers that he does not speak dogmatically in anything that he says, but that he intends simply to present the Sceptical arguments historically, and as they appear to him. He characterizes his treatment of the subject as general rather than critical, including a statement of the character of Scepticism, its idea, its principles, its manner of reasoning, its criterion and aim, and a presentation of the Tropes, or aspects of doubt, and the Sceptical formulae and the distinction between Scepticism and the related schools of philosophy.[1]

The result of all the gradual changes which the development of thought had brought about in the outward relations of the Sceptical School, was to increase the earnestness of the claim of the Sceptics to be simply followers of Pyrrho, the great founder of the movement. In discussing the names given to the Sceptics, Sextus gives precedence very decidedly to the title "Pyrrhonean," because Pyrrho appears the best representative of Scepticism, and more prominent than all who before him occupied themselves with it.[2]

It was a question much discussed among philosophers in ancient times, whether Pyrrhonism should be considered a philosophical sect or not. Thus we find that Hippobotus in his work entitled

[Greek: peri haireseon], written shortly before our era, does not include Pyrrhonism among the other sects.[3] Diogenes himself, after some hesitation remarking that many do not consider it a sect, finally decides to call it so.[4]

[1] *Hyp.* I. 5, 6.

[2] *Hyp.* I. 7.

[3] Diog. *Pro.* 19.

[4] Diog. *Pro.* 20.

Sextus in discussing this subject calls Scepticism an [Greek: agoge], or a movement, rather than a [Greek: hairesis], saying that Scepticism is not a sect, if that word implies a systematic arrangement of dogmas, for the Sceptic has no dogmas. If, however, a sect may mean simply the following of a certain system of reasoning according to what appears to be true, then Scepticism is a sect.[1] From a quotation given later on by Sextus from Aenesidemus, we know that the latter used the term [Greek: agoge].[2] Sextus gives also the other titles, so well known as having been applied to Scepticism, namely, [Greek: zetetike], [Greek: ephektike], and [Greek: aporetike].[3] The [Greek: dunamis][4] of Scepticism is to oppose the things of sense and intellect in every possible way to each other, and through the equal weight of things opposed, or [Greek: isostheneia], to reach first the state of suspension of judgement, and afterwards ataraxia, or "repose and tranquillity of soul."[5] The purpose of Scepticism is then the hope of ataraxia, and its origin was in the troubled state of mind induced by the inequality of things, and uncertainty in regard to the truth. Therefore, says Sextus, men of the greatest talent began the Sceptical system by placing in opposition to every argument an equal one, thus leading to a philosophical system without a dogma, for the Sceptic claims that he has no dogma.[6] The Sceptic is never supposed to state a decided opinion, but only to say what appears to him. Even the Sceptical formulae, such as "Nothing more,"[7] or "I decide nothing,"[8] or "All is false," include themselves with other things. The only statements that the Sceptic can make, are in regard to his own sensations. He cannot deny that he is warm or cold or hungry.

[1] *Hyp.* I. 15, 17.

[2] *Hyp.* I. 210.

[3] *Hyp.* I. 7; Diog. IX. 11, 70.

[4] *Hyp.* I. 8.

[5] *Hyp.* I. 10.

[6] *Hyp.* I. 12.

[7] *Hyp.* I. 14.

[8] *Hyp.* I. 14.

Sextus replies to the charge that the Sceptics deny phenomena by refuting it.[1] The Sceptic does not deny phenomena, because they are the only criteria by which he can regulate his actions. "We call the criterion of the Sceptical School the phenomenon, meaning by this name the idea of it."[2] Phenomena are the only things which the Sceptic does not deny, and he guides his life by them. They are, however, subjective. Sextus distinctly affirms that sensations are the phenomena,[3] and that they lie in susceptibility and voluntary feeling, and that they constitute the appearances of objects.[4] We see from this that Sextus makes the only reality to consist in subjective experience, but he does not follow this to its logical conclusion, and doubt the existence of anything outside of mind. He rather takes for granted that there is a something unknown outside, about which the Sceptic can make no assertions. Phenomena are the criteria according to which the Sceptic orders his daily life, as he cannot be entirely inactive, and they affect life in four different ways. They constitute the guidance of nature, the impulse of feeling; they give rise to the traditions of customs and laws, and make the teaching of the arts important.[5] According to the tradition of laws and customs, piety is a good in daily life, but it is not in itself an abstract good. The Sceptic of Sextus' time also inculcated the teaching of the arts, as indeed must be the case with professing physicians, as most of the leading Sceptics were. Sextus says, "We are not without energy in the arts which we undertake."[6] This was a positive tendency which no philosophy, however negative, could escape, and the Sceptic tried to avoid inconsistency in this respect, by separating his philosophy from his theory of life. His philosophy controlled his opinions, and his life was governed by phenomena.

[1] *Hyp.* I. 19.

[2] *Hyp.* I. 19.

[3] *Hyp.* I. 22; Diog. IX. 11, 105.

[4] *Hyp.* I. 22.

[5] *Hyp.* I. 23.

[6] *Hyp.* I. 24.

The aim of Pyrrhonism was ataraxia in those things which pertain to opinion, and moderation in the things which life imposes.[1] In other words, we find here the same natural desire of the human being to rise above and beyond the limitations which pain and passion impose, which is expressed in other forms, and under other names, in other schools of philosophy. The method, however, by which ataraxia or peace of mind could be reached, was peculiar to the Sceptic. It is a state of psychological equilibrium, which results from the equality of the weight of different arguments that are opposed to each other, and the consequent impossibility of affirming in regard to either one, that it is correct.[2] The discovery of ataraxia was, in the first instance, apparently accidental, for while the Sceptic withheld his opinion, unable to decide what things were true, and what things were false, ataraxia fortunately followed.[3] After he had begun to philosophize, with a desire to discriminate in regard to ideas, and to separate the true from the false[4] during the time of [Greek: epoche], or suspension of judgement, ataraxia followed as if by chance, as the shadow follows the body.[5]

[1] *Hyp.* I. 25.

[2] *Hyp.* I. 26.

[3] *Hyp.* I. 26.

[4] Diog. IX. 11, 107.

[5] *Hyp.* I. 29.

The Sceptic in seeking ataraxia in the things of opinion, does not entirely escape from suffering from his sensations. He is not wholly undisturbed, for he is sometimes cold and hungry, and so on.[1] He claims, nevertheless, that he suffers less than the dogmatist, who is beset with two kinds of suffering, one from the feelings themselves, and also from the conviction that they are by nature an evil.[2] To the Sceptic nothing is in itself either an evil or a good, and so he thinks that "he escapes from difficulties easier."[3] For instance, he who considers riches a good in themselves, is unhappy in the loss of them, and in possession of them is in fear of losing them, while the Sceptic, remembering the Sceptical saying "No more," is untroubled in whatever condition he may be found, as the loss of riches is no more an evil than the possession of them is a good.[4] For he who considers anything good or bad by nature is always troubled, and when that which seemed good is not present with him, he thinks that he is tortured by that which is by nature bad, and follows after what he thinks to be good. Having acquired it, however, he is not at rest, for his reason tells him that a sudden change may deprive him of this thing that he considers a good.[5] The Sceptic, however, endeavours neither to avoid nor seek anything eagerly.[6]

[1] *Hyp.* I. 30.

[2] *Hyp.* I. 30.

[3] *Hyp.* I. 30; Diog. IX. 11, 61.

[4] *Adv. Math.* XI. 146-160.

[5] *Hyp.* I. 27.

[6] *Hyp.* I. 28.

Ataraxia came to the Sceptic as success in painting the foam on a horse's mouth came to Apelles the painter. After many attempts to do this, and many failures, he gave up in despair, and threw the sponge at the picture that he had used to wipe the colors from the painting with. As soon as it touched the picture it produced a representation of the foam.[1] Thus the Sceptics were never able to attain to ataraxia by examining the anomaly between the phenomena and the things of thought, but it came to them of its own accord just when they despaired of finding it.

The intellectual preparation for producing ataraxia, consists in placing arguments in opposition to each other, both in regard to phenomena, and to things of the intellect. By placing the phenomenal in opposition to the phenomenal, the intellectual to the intellectual, and the phenomenal to the intellectual, and *vice versa*, the present to the present, past, and future, one will find that no argument exists that is incontrovertible. It is not necessary to accept any statement whatever as true, and consequently a state of [Greek: epoche] may always be maintained.[2] Although ataraxia concerns things of the opinion, and must be preceded by the intellectual process described above, it is not itself a function of the intellect, or any subtle kind of reasoning, but seems to be rather a unique form of moral perfection, leading to happiness, or is itself happiness.

[1] *Hyp.* I. 28, 29.

[2] *Hyp.* I. 32-35.

It was the aim of Scepticism to know nothing, and to assert nothing in regard to any subject, but at the same time not to affirm that knowledge on all subjects is impossible, and consequently to have the attitude of still seeking. The standpoint of Pyrrhonism was materialistic. We find from the teachings of Sextus that he affirmed the non-existence of the soul,[1] or the ego, and denied absolute existence altogether.[2] The introductory statements of Diogenes regarding Pyrrhonism would agree with this standpoint.[3]

There is no criterion of truth in Scepticism. We cannot prove that the phenomena represent objects, or find out what the relation of phenomena to objects is. There is no criterion to tell us which one is true of all the different representations of the same object, and of all the varieties of sensation that arise through the many phases of relativity of the conditions which control the character of the phenomena.

Every effort to find the truth can deal only with phenomena, and absolute reality can never be known.

[1] ***Adv. Math.*** VII. 55; ***Hyp.*** II. 32.

[2] ***Adv. Math.*** XI. 140.

[3] Diog. IX. 11, 61.

CHAPTER III.

The Sceptical Tropes.

The exposition of the Tropes of Pyrrhonism constitutes historically and philosophically the most important part of the writings of Sextus Empiricus. These Tropes represent the sum total of the wisdom of the older Sceptical School, and were held in high respect for centuries, not only by the Pyrrhoneans, but also by many outside the narrow limits of that School. In the first book of the ***Hypotyposes*** Sextus gives two classes of Tropes, those of [Greek: epoche] and the eight Tropes of Aenesidemus against Aetiology.

The Tropes of [Greek: epoche] are arranged in groups of ten, five and two, according to the period of the Sceptical School to which they belong; the first of these groups is historically the most important, or the Ten Tropes of [Greek: epoche], as these are far more closely connected with the general development of Scepticism, than the later ones. By the name [Greek: tropos] or Trope, the Sceptic understood a manner of thought, or form of argument, or standpoint of judgement. It was a term common in Greek philosophy, used in this sense, from the time of Aristotle.[1] The Stoics, however, used the word with a different meaning from that attributed to it by the Sceptics.[2] Stephanus and Fabricius translate it by the Latin word ***modus***[3] and [Greek: tropos] also is often used interchangeably with the word [Greek: logos] by Sextus, Diogenes Laertius, and others; sometimes also as synonymous with [Greek:

topos],[4] and [Greek: typos] is found in the oldest edition of Sextus.[5] Diogenes defines the word as the standpoint, or manner of argument, by which the Sceptics arrived at the condition of doubt, in consequence of the equality of probabilities, and he calls the Tropes, the ten Tropes of doubt.[6] All writers on Pyrrhonism after the time of Aenesidemus give the Tropes the principal place in their treatment of the subject. Sextus occupies two thirds of the first book of the *Hypotyposes* in stating and discussing them; and about one fourth of his presentation of Scepticism is devoted to the Tropes by Diogenes. In addition to these two authors, Aristocles the Peripatetic refers to them in his attack on Scepticism.[7] Favorinus wrote a book entitled Pyrrhonean Tropes*, and Plutarch one called* The Ten ([Greek: topoi]) Topes of Pyrrho.[8] Both of these latter works are lost.

[1] Pappenheim *Erlauterung Pyrrh. Grundzugen*, p. 35.

[2] Diog I. 76; *Adv. Math.* VIII. 227.

[3] Fabricius, Cap. XIV. 7.

[4] *Hyp.* I. 36.

[5] Fabricius on *Hyp.* I. 36; Cap. XIV. G.

[6] Diog. IX. 11, 79-108.

[7] Aristocles *Euseb. praep. ev.* X. 14, 18.

[8] Fabricius on *Hyp.* I. 36.

All authorities unite in attributing to Aenesidemus the work of systematizing and presenting to the world the ten Tropes of [Greek: epoche]. He was the first to conceive the project of opposing an organized philosophical system of Pyrrhonism to the dogmatism of his contemporaries.[1] Moreover, the fact that Diogenes introduces the Tropes into his life of Pyrrho, does not necessarily imply that he considered Pyrrho their author, for Diogenes invariably combines the teachings of the followers of a movement with those of the founders themselves; he gives these Tropes after speaking of Aenesidemus' work entitled Pyrrhonean Hypotyposes, and apparently quotes from this book, in giving at least a part of his presentation of Pyrrhonism, either directly or through, the works of others. Nietzsche proposes a correction of the text of Diogenes IX. 11, 79, which would make him quote the Tropes from a book by Theodosius,[2] author of a commentary on the works of Theodas. No writer of antiquity claims for the Tropes an older source than the books of Aenesidemus, to whom Aristocles also attributes them.[3] They are not mentioned in Diogenes' life of Timon, the immediate disciple of Pyrrho. Cicero has no knowledge of them, and does not refer to them in his discussion of Scepticism.

[1] Compare Saisset *Op. cit.* p. 78.

[2] Brochard *Op. cit.* 254, Note 4.

[3] Aristocles *Eus. praep. ev.* XIV. 18. 8.

Aenesidemus was undoubtedly the first to formulate these Tropes, but many things tend to show that they resulted, in reality, from the gradual classification of the results of the teachings of Pyrrho, in the subsequent development of thought from his own time to that of Aenesidemus. The ideas contained in the Tropes were not original with Aenesidemus, but are more closely connected with the thought of earlier times. The decidedly empirical character of the Tropes proves this connection, for the eight Tropes of Aetiology, which were original with Aenesidemus, bear a far stronger dialectic stamp, thus showing a more decided dialectic influence of the Academy than is found in the Tropes of [Greek: epoche]. Many of the illustrations given of the Tropes also, testify to a time of greater antiquity than that of Aenesidemus. The name Trope was well known in ancient times, and the number ten reminds us of the ten opposing principles of Pythagoras, and the ten categories of Aristotle, the fourth of which was the same as the eighth Trope. The terminology, however, with very few exceptions, points to a later period than that of Pyrrho. Zeller points out a number of expressions in both Diogenes' and Sextus' exposition of the Tropes, which could not date back farther than the time of Aenesidemus.[1] One of the most striking features of the whole presentation of the Tropes, especially as given by Sextus, is their mosaic character, stamping them not as the work of one person, but as a growth, and also an agglutinous growth, lacking very decidedly the symmetry of thought that the work of one mind would have shown.

[1] Zeller *Op. cit.* p. 25.

At the time of the separation of Pyrrhonism from the Academy, no other force was as strong in giving life to the school as the systematic treatment by Aenesidemus of the Ten Tropes of [Greek: epoche]. The reason of this is evident. It was not that the ideas of the Sceptical Tropes were original with Aenesidemus, but because a definite statement of belief is always a far more powerful influence than principles which are vaguely understood and accepted. There is always, however, the danger to the

Sceptic, in making a statement even of the principles of Scepticism, that the psychological result would be a dogmatic tendency of mind, as we shall see later was the case, even with Aenesidemus himself. That the Sceptical School could not escape the accusation of dogmatizing, from the Dogmatics, even in stating the grounds of their Scepticism, we know from Diogenes.[1] To avoid this dogmatic tendency of the ten Tropes, Sextus makes the frequent assertion that he does not affirm things to be absolutely true, but states them as they appear to him, and that they may be otherwise from what he has said.[2]

[1] Diog. IX. 11, 102.

[2] *Hyp.* I. 4, 24.

Sextus tells us that "Certain Tropes, ten in number, for producing the state of [Greek: epoche] have been handed down from the older Sceptics."[1] He refers to them in another work as the "Tropes of Aenesidemus."[2] There is no evidence that the substance of these Tropes was changed after the time of Aenesidemus, although many of the illustrations given by Sextus must have been of a later date, added during the two centuries that elapsed between the time of Aenesidemus and Sextus. In giving these Tropes Sextus does not claim to offer a systematic methodical classification, and closes his list of them, in their original concise form, with the remark, "We make this order ourselves."[3] The order is given differently by Diogenes, and also by Favorinus.[4] The Trope which Sextus gives as the tenth is the fifth given by Diogenes, the seventh by Sextus is the eighth given by Diogenes, the fifth by Sextus, the seventh by Diogenes, the tenth by Diogenes, the eighth by Sextus. Diogenes says that the one he gives as the ninth Favorinus calls the eighth, and Sextus and Aenesidemus the tenth. This statement does not correspond with the list of the Tropes which Sextus gives, proving that Diogenes took some other text than that of Sextus as his authority.[5] The difference in the order of the Tropes shows, also, that the order was not considered a matter of great importance. There is a marked contrast in the spirit of the two presentations of the Tropes given by Sextus and Diogenes. The former gives them not only as an orator, but as one who feels that he is defending his own cause, and the school of which he is the leader, against mortal enemies, while Diogenes relates them as an historian.

[1] *Hyp.* I. 36.

[2] *Adv. Math.* VII. 345.

[3] *Hyp.* I. 38.

[4] Diog. IX. 11, 87.

[5] Diog. IX. 11, 87.

Pappenheim tries to prove[1] that Aenesidemus originally gave only nine Tropes in his *Pyrrhonean Hypotyposes*, as Aristocles mentions only nine in referring to the Tropes of Aenesidemus, and that the tenth was added later. Had this been the case, however, the fact would surely have been mentioned either by Diogenes or Sextus, who both refer to the ten Tropes of Aenesidemus.

The Tropes claim to prove that the character of phenomena is so relative and changeable, that certain knowledge cannot be based upon them, and as we have shown, there is no other criterion of knowledge for the Sceptic than phenomena.[2] All of the Tropes, except the tenth, are connected with sense-perception, and relate to the difference of the results obtained through the senses under different circumstances. They may be divided into two classes, *i.e.*, those based upon differences of our physical organism, and those based upon external differences. To the first class belong the first, second, third and fourth; to the second class, the fifth, sixth, seventh and eighth, and also the ninth. The eighth, or that of relation, is applied objectively both by Sextus and Diogenes in their treatment of the Tropes, and is not used for objects of thought alone, but principally to show the relation of outward objects to each other. The tenth is the only one which has a moral significance, and it has also a higher subjective value than the others; it takes its arguments from an entirely different sphere of thought, and deals with metaphysical and religious contradictions in opinion, and with the question of good and evil. That this Trope is one of the oldest, we know from its distinct mention in connection with the foundation theories of Pyrrho, by Diogenes.[3] In treating of the subjective reasons for doubt as to the character of external reality, the Sceptics were very near the denial of all outward reality, a point, however, which they never quite reached.

[1] Pappenheim, *Die Tropen der Griechen*, p. 23.

[2] *Hyp.* I. 22.

[3] Diog. IX. 11, 61.

There is evidently much of Sextus' own thought mixed with the illustrations of the Tropes, but it is impossible to separate the original parts from the material that was the common property of the Sceptical School. Many of these illustrations show, however, perfect familiarity with the scientific and medical teachings of the time. Before entering upon his exposition of the Tropes, Sextus gives them in the short concise form in which they must first have existed[1]--

(i) Based upon the variety of animals.

(ii) Based upon the differences between men.

(iii) Based upon differences in the constitution of the sense organs.

(iv) Based upon circumstances.

(v) Based upon position, distance and place.

(vi) Based upon mixtures.

(vii) Based upon the quantities and constitutions of objects.

(viii) Relation.

(ix) Based upon frequency or rarity of occurences.

(x) Based upon systems, customs and laws, mythical beliefs, and dogmatic opinions.

[1] *Hyp.* I. 36-38.

Although Sextus is careful not to dogmatise regarding the arrangement of the Tropes, yet there is in his classification of them a regular gradation, from the arguments based upon differences in animals to those in man, first considering the latter in relation to the physical constitution, and then to circumstances outside of us, and finally the treatment of metaphysical and moral differences.

The First Trope.[1] That the same mental representations are not found in different animals, may be inferred from their differences in constitution resulting from their different origins, and from the variety in their organs of sense. Sextus takes up the five senses in order, giving illustrations to prove the relative results of the mental representations in all of them, as for example the subjectivity of color[2] and sound.[3] All knowledge of objects through the senses is relative and not absolute. Sextus does not, accordingly, confine the impossibility of certain knowledge to the qualities that Locke regards as secondary, but includes also the primary ones in this statement.[4] The form and shape of objects as they appear to us may be changed by pressure on the eyeball. Furthermore, the character of reflections in mirrors depend entirely on their shape, as the images in concave mirrors are very different from those in convex ones; and so in the same way as the eyes of animals are of different shapes, and supplied with different fluids, the ideas of dogs, fishes, men and grasshoppers must be very different.[5]

[1] *Hyp.*. I. 40-61.

[2] *Hyp.*. I. 44-46.

[3] *Hyp.*. I. 50.

[4] *Hyp.*. I. 47.

[5] *Hyp.*. I. 49.

In discussing the mental representations of animals of different grades of intelligence, Sextus shows a very good comprehension of the philogenetic development of the organs of sense, and draws the final conclusion that external objects are regarded differently by animals, according to their difference in constitution.[1] These differences in the ideas which different animals have of the same objects are demonstrated by their different tastes, as the things desired by some are fatal to others.[2] The practical illustrations given of this result show a familiarity with natural history, and cognizance of the tastes and habits of many animals,[3] but were probably few of them original with Sextus, unless perhaps in their application; that this train of reasoning was the common property of the Sceptic School, we know from the fact that Diogenes begins his exposition of the first Trope in a way similar to that of Sextus.[4] His illustrations are, however, few and meagre compared with those of Sextus, and the scientific facts used by both of them may mostly be found in other authors of antiquity given in a similar way.[5] The logical result of the reasoning used to explain the first Trope, is that we cannot compare the ideas of the animals with each other, nor with our own; nor can we prove that our ideas are more trustworthy than those of the animals.[6] As therefore an examination of ideas is impossible, any decided opinion about their trustworthiness is also impossible, and this Trope leads to the suspension of judgment regarding external objects, or to [Greek: epoche.][7]

[1] *Hyp.*. I. 54.

[2] *Hyp.*. I. 55.

[3] *Hyp.*. I. 55-59.

[4] Diog. IX. 11, 79-80.

[5] Pappenheim *Erlauterung Pyrr. Grundzuege Par*. 41.

[6] *Hyp*. I. 59.

[7] *Hyp*. I. 61.

After reaching this conclusion, Sextus introduces a long chapter to prove that animals can reason. There is no reference to this in Diogenes, but there is other testimony to show that it was a favourite line of argument with the Sceptics.[1] Sextus, however, says that his course of reasoning is different from that of most of the Sceptics on the subject,[2] as they usually applied their arguments to all animals, while he selected only one, namely the dog.[3] This chapter is full of sarcastic attacks on the Dogmatics, and contains the special allusion to the Stoics as the greatest opponents of the Sceptics, which has been before referred to.[4]

Sextus claims with a greater freedom of diction than in some apparently less original chapters, and with a wealth of special illustrations, that the dog is superior to man in acuteness of perception,[5] that he has the power of choice, and possesses an art, that of hunting,[6] and, also, is not deprived of virtue,[7] as the true nature of virtue is to show justice to all, which the dog does by guarding loyally those who are kind to him, and keeping off those who do evil.[8] The reasoning power of this animal is proved by the story taken from Chrysippus, of the dog that came to a meeting of three roads in following a scent. After seeking the scent in vain in two of the roads, he takes the third road without scenting it as a result of a quick process of thought, which proves that he shares in the famous dialectic of Chrysippus,[9] the five forms of [Greek: *anapodeiktoi logoi*,] of which the dog chooses the fifth. Either *A* or *B* or *C*, not *A* or *B,* therefore *C*.

[1] *Hyp*. I. 238.

[2] Compare Brochard *Op. cit.* 256.

[3] *Hyp*. I. 62-63.

[4] *Hyp*. I. 65.

[5] *Hyp*. I. 64.

[6] *Hyp*. I. 66.

[7] *Hyp*. I. 67.

[8] *Hyp*. I. 67.

[9] *Hyp*. I. 69; *Hyp*. II. 166; Diog. VII. 1, 79.

The dog and other irrational animals may also possess spoken language, as the only proof that we have to the contrary, is the fact that we cannot understand the sounds that they make.[1] We have an example in this chapter of the humor of Sextus, who after enlarging on the perfect character of the dog, remarks, "For which reason it seems to me some philosophers have honoured themselves with the name of this animal,"[2] thus making a sarcastic allusion to the Cynics, especially Antisthenes.[3]

[1] *Hyp*. I. 74.

[2] *Hyp*. I. 72.

[3] Diog. VI. 1, 13.

The Second Trope. Passing on to the second Trope, Sextus aims to prove that even if we leave the differences of the mental images of animals out of the discussion, there is not a sufficient unanimity in the mental images of human beings to allow us to base any assertions upon them in regard to the character of external objects.[1] He had previously announced that he intended to oppose the phenomenal to the intellectual "in any way whatever,"[2] so he begins here by referring to the two parts of which man is said to be composed, the soul and the body, and proceeds to discuss the differences among men in sense-perception and in opinion.[3] Most of the illustrations given of differences in sense-perception are medical ones; of the more general of these I will note the only two which are also given by Diogenes in his exposition of this Trope,[4] viz., Demophon, Alexander's table waiter, who shivered in the sun, and Andron the Argive, who was so free from thirst that he travelled through the desert of Libya without seeking a drink. Some have reasoned from the presence of the first of these illustrations in the exposition of the Tropes, that a part of this material at least goes back to the time of Pyrrho, as Pyrrho from his intimacy with Alexander, when he accompanied him to India, had abundant opportunities to observe the peculiarities of his servant Demophon.[5] The illustration of Andron the Argive is taken from Aristotle, according to Diogenes.[6]

[1] *Hyp*. I. 79.

[2] *Hyp.* I. 8.

[3] *Hyp.* I. 80.

[4] Diog. IX. 11, 80-81.

[5] Compare Pyrrhon et le Scepticism primitive, Revue phil., Paris 1885, No. 5; Victor Brochard, p. 521.

[6] Diog. IX. 11, 81.

Passing on to differences of opinion, we have another example of the sarcastic humor of Sextus, as he refers to the [Greek: physiognomonike sophia][1] as the authority for believing that the body is a type of the soul. As the bodies of men differ, so the souls also probably differ. The differences of mind among men is not referred to by Diogenes, except in the general statement that they choose different professions; while Sextus elaborates this point, speaking of the great differences in opposing schools of philosophy, and in the objects of choice and avoidance, and sources of pleasure for different men.[2] The poets well understand this marked difference in human desires, as Homer says,

"One man enjoys this, another enjoys that."

Sextus also quotes the beautiful lines of Pindar,[3]

"One delights in getting honours and crowns through stormfooted horses,
Others in passing life in rooms rich in gold,
Another safe travelling enjoys, in a swift ship,

on a wave of the sea."

[1] *Hyp.* I. 85.

[2] *Hyp.* I. 87-89.

[3] *Hyp.* I. 86.

The Third Trope. The third Trope limits the argument to the sense-perceptions of one man, a Dogmatic, if preferred, or to one whom the Dogmatics consider wise,[1] and states that as the ideas given by the different sense organs differ radically in a way that does not admit of their being compared with each other, they furnish no reliable testimony regarding the nature of objects.[2] "Each of the phenomena perceived by us seems to present itself in many forms, as the apple, smooth, fragrant brown and sweet." The apple was evidently the ordinary example given for this Trope, for Diogenes uses the same, but in a much more condensed form, and not with equal understanding of the results to be deduced from it.[3] The consequence of the incompatibility of the mental representations produced through the several sense organs by the apple, may be the acceptance of either of the three following propositions: (i) That only those qualities exist in the apple which we perceive. (ii) That more than these exist. (iii) That even those perceived do not exist.[4] Accordingly, any experience which can give rise to such different views regarding outward objects, cannot be relied upon as a testimony concerning them.

[1] *Hyp.* I. 90.

[2] *Hyp.* I. 94.

[3] Diog. IX. 11 81.

[4] *Hyp.* I. 99.

The non-homogeneous nature of the mental images connected with the different sense organs, as presented by Sextus, reminds us of the discussion of the same subject by Berkeley in his Theory of Vision.

Sextus says that a man born with less than the usual number of senses, would form altogether different ideas of the external world than those who have the usual number, and as our ideas of objects depend on our mental images, a greater number of sense organs would give us still different ideas of outward reality.[1] The strong argument of the Stoics against such reasoning as this, was their doctrine of pre-established harmony between nature and the soul, so that when a representation is produced in us of a real object, a [Greek: kataleptike phantasia],[2] by this representation the soul grasps a real existence. There is a [Greek: logos] in us which is of the same kind, [Greek: syngenos], or in relation to all nature. This argument of pre-established harmony between the faculties of the soul and the objects of nature, is the one that has been used in all ages to combat philosophical teaching that denies that we apprehend the external world as it is. It was used against Kant by his opponents, who thought in this way to refute his teachings.[3] The Sceptics could not, of course, accept a theory of nature that included the soul and the external world in one harmonious whole, but Sextus in his discussion of the third Trope does not refute this argument as fully as he does later in his work against logic.[4] He simply states here that philosophers themselves cannot agree as to what nature is, and furthermore, that a philosopher himself is a part of the discord, and to be judged, rather than being capable of judging, and that no conclusion can be reached by those who are themselves an element of the uncertainty.[5]

[1] *Hyp.* I. 96-97.

[2] *Adv. Math.* VII. 93.

[3] Ueberweg *Op. cit.* 195.

[4] *Adv. Math.* VII. 354.

[5] *Hyp.* I. 98-99.

The Fourth Trope. This Trope limits the argument to each separate sense, and the effect is considered of the condition of body and mind upon sense-perception in relation to the several sense-organs.[1] The physical states which modify sense-perception are health and illness, sleeping and waking, youth and age, hunger and satiety, drunkenness and sobriety. All of these conditions of the body entirely change the character of the mental images, producing different judgments of the color, taste, and temperature of objects, and of the character of sounds. A man who is asleep is in a different world from one awake, the existence of both worlds being relative to the condition of waking and sleeping.[2]

The subjective states which Sextus mentions here as modifying the character of the mental representations are hating or loving, courage or fear, sorrow or joy, and sanity or insanity.[3] No man is ever twice in exactly the same condition of body or mind, and never able to review the differences of his ideas as a sum total, for those of the present moment only are subject to careful inspection.[4] Furthermore, no one is free from the influence of all conditions of body or mind, so that he can be unbiassed to judge his ideas, and no criterion can be established that can be shown to be true, but on the contrary, whatever course is pursued on the subject, both the criterion and the proof will be thrown into the *circulus in probando*, for the truth of each rests on the other.[5]

[1] *Hyp.* I. 100.

[2] *Hyp.* I. 104.

[3] *Hyp.* I. 100.

[4] *Hyp.* I. 112.

[5] *Hyp.* I. 117.

Diogenes gives in part the same illustrations of this Trope, but in a much more condensed form. The marked characteristic of this train of reasoning is the attempt to prove that abnormal conditions are also natural. In referring at first to the opposing states of body and mind, which so change the character of sense-perception, Sextus classifies them according to the popular usage as [Greek: kata physin] and [Greek: para physin]. This distinction was an important one, even with Aristotle, and was especially developed by the Stoics[1] in a broader sense than referring merely to health and sickness. The Stoics, however, considered only normal conditions as being according to nature. Sextus, on the contrary, declares that abnormal states are also conditions according to nature,[2] and just as those who are in health are in a state that is natural to those who are in health, so also those not in health are in a state that is natural to those not in health, and in some respects according to nature. Existence, then, and non-existence are not absolute, but relative, and the world of sleep as really exists for those who are asleep as the things that exist in waking exist, although they do not exist in sleep.[3] One mental representation, therefore, cannot be judged by another, which is also in a state of relation to existing physical and mental conditions. Diogenes states this principle even more decidedly in his exposition of this Trope. "The insane are not in a condition opposed to nature; why they more than we? For we also see the sun as if it were stationary."[4] Furthermore, in different periods of life ideas differ. Children are fond of balls and hoops, while those in their prime prefer other things, and the aged still others.[5] The wisdom contained in this Trope in reference to the relative value of the things most sought after is not original with Sextus, but is found in the more earnest ethical teachings of older writers. Sextus does not, however, draw any moral conclusions from this reasoning, but only uses it as an argument for [Greek: epoche].

[1] Diog. VII. 1, 86.

[2] *Hyp.* I. 103.

[3] *Hyp.* I. 104.

[4] Diog. IX. 11, 82.

[5] *Hyp.* I. 106.

The Fifth Trope. This Trope leaves the discussion of the dependence of the ideas upon the physical nature, and takes up the influence of the environment upon them. It makes the difference in ideas depend upon the position, distance, and place of objects, thus taking apparently their real existence for granted. Things change their form and shape according to the distance from which they are observed, and the position in which they stand.[1]

The same light or tone alters decidedly in different surroundings. Perspective in paintings depends on the angle at which the picture is suspended.[2] With Diogenes this Trope is the seventh,[3] and his exposition of it is similar, but as usual, shorter. Both Sextus and Diogenes give the illustration[4] of the neck of the dove differing in color in different degrees of inclination, an illustration used by Protagoras also to prove the relativity of perception by the senses. "The black neck of the dove in the shade appears black, but in the light sunny and purple."[5] Since, then, all phenomena are regarded in a certain place, and from a certain distance, and according to a certain position, each of which relations makes a great difference with the mental images, we shall be obliged also by this Trope to come to the reserving of the opinion.[6]

[1] *Hyp.* I. 118.

[2] *Hyp.* I. 120.

[3] Diog. IX. 11, 85.

[4] *Hyp.* I. 120; Diog. IX. 11, 86.

[5] *Schol. zu Arist.* 60, 18, ed. Brandis; Pappen. Er. Pyrr. Grundzuege, p. 54.

[6] *Hyp.* I. 121.

The Sixth Trope. This Trope leads to [Greek: epoche] regarding the nature of objects, because no object can ever be presented to the organs of sense directly, but must always be perceived through some medium, or in some mixture.[1] This mixture may be an outward one, connected with the temperature, or the rarity of the air, or the water[2] surrounding an object, or it may be a mixture resulting from the different humors of the sense-organs.[3] A man with the jaundice, for example, sees colors differently from one who is in health. The illustration of the jaundice is a favorite one with the Sceptics. Diogenes uses it several times in his presentation of Scepticism, and it occurs in Sextus' writings in all, as an illustration, in eight different places.[4] The condition of the organ of the [Greek: hegemonikon], or the ruling faculty, may also cause mixtures. Pappenheim thinks that we have here Kant's idea of ***a priori***, only on a materialistic foundation.[5] A careful consideration of the passage, however, shows us that Sextus' thought is more in harmony with the discoveries of modern psychiatry than with the philosophy of Kant. If the sentence, [Greek: isos de kai aute (he dianoia) epimixian tina idian poieitai pros ta hypo ton aistheseon anangellomena],[6] stood alone, without further explanation, it might well refer to ***a priori*** laws of thought, but the explanation which follows beginning with "because" makes that impossible.[7] "Because in each of the places where the Dogmatics think that the ruling faculty is, we see present certain humors, which are the cause of mixtures." Sextus does not advance any opinion as to the place of the ruling faculty in the body, which is, according to the Stoics, the principal part of the soul, where ideas, desires, and reasoning originate,[8] but simply refers to the two theories of the Dogmatics, which claim on the one hand that it is in the brain, and on the other that it is in the heart.[9] This subject he deals with more fully in his work against logic.[10] As, however, he bases his argument, in discussing possible intellectual mixtures in illustration of the sixth Trope, entirely on the condition of the organ of the intellect, it is evident that his theory of the soul was a materialistic one.

[1] *Hyp.* I. 124.

[2] *Hyp.* I. 125.

[3] *Hyp.* I. 126.

[4] See Index to Bekker's edition of Sextus.

[5] Papp. *Er. Pyr. Gr.* p. 55.

[6] *Hyp.* I. 128.

[7] *Hyp.* I. 128.

[8] Diog. VII. 1, 159.

[9] *Hyp.* I. 128.

[10] *Adv. Math.* VII. 313.

The Seventh Trope. This Trope, based upon the quantities and compositions of objects, is illustrated by examples of different kinds of food, drink, and medicine, showing the different effects according to the quantity taken, as the harmfulness and the usefulness of most things depend on their quantity. Things act differently upon the senses if applied in small or large quantities, as filings of metal or horn, and separate grains of sand have a different color and touch from the same taken in the form of a solid.[1] The result is that ideas vary according to the composition of the object, and this Trope also brings to confusion the existence of outward objects, and leads us to reserve our opinion in regard to them.[2] This Trope is illustrated by Diogenes with exceeding brevity.[3]

[1] *Hyp.* I. 129-131.

[2] *Hyp.* I. 134.

[3] Diog. IX. 11, 86.

The Eighth Trope. The Trope based upon relation contains, as Sextus rightly remarks, the substance of the other nine,[1] for the general statement of the relativity of knowledge includes the other statements made. The prominence which Sextus gave this Trope in his introduction to the ten Tropes leads one to expect here new illustrations and added[2] arguments for [Greek: epoche]. We find, however, neither of these, but simply a statement that all things are in relation in one of two ways, either directly, or as being a part of a difference. These two kinds of relation are given by Protagoras, and might have been used to good purpose in the introduction to the Tropes, or at the end, to prove that all the others were really subordinate to the eighth. The reasoning is, however simply applied to the relation of objects to each other, and nothing is added that is not found elsewhere where as an argument for [Greek: epoche].[3] This Trope is the tenth by Diogenes, and he strengthens his reasoning in regard to it, by a statement that Sextus does not directly make, *i.e.*, that everything is in relation to the understanding.[4]

[1] *Hyp.* I. 39.

[2] *Hyp.* I. 135-140.

[3] *Hyp.* I. 135-140.

[4] Diog. IX. 11, 88.

The Ninth Trope. This is based upon the frequency and rarity of events, and refers to some of the phenomena of nature, such as the rising of the sun, and the sea, as no longer a source of astonishment, while a comet or an earthquake are wonders to those not accustomed to them.[1] The value of objects also depends on their rarity, as for example the value of gold.[2] Furthermore, things may be valuable at one time, and at another not so, according to the frequency and rarity of the occurrence.[3] Therefore this Trope also leads to [Greek: epoche]. Diogenes gives only two illustrations to this Trope, that of the sun and the earthquake.[4]

[1] *Hyp.* I. 141-142.

[2] *Hyp.* I. 143.

[3] *Hyp.* I. 144.

[4] Diog. IX. 11, 87.

The Tenth Trope. We have already remarked on the difference in the character of the tenth Trope, dealing as it does, not with the ideas of objects, like the other nine Tropes, but with philosophical and religious opinions, and questions of right and wrong. It was the well-known aim of the Sceptics to submit to the laws and customs of the land where they were found, and to conform to certain moral teachings and religious ceremonies; this they did without either affirming or denying the truth of the principles upon which these teachings were based,[1] and also without any passion or strong feeling in regard to them,[2] as nothing in itself can be proved to be good or evil. The tenth Trope accordingly, brings forward contradictions in customs, laws, and the beliefs of different lands, to show that they are also changeable and relative, and not of absolute worth. The foundation-thought of this Trope is given twice by Diogenes, once as we have before stated in his introduction[3] to the life of Pyrrho, and also as one of the Tropes.[4] As it is apparently one of the oldest of the Tropes, it would naturally be much used in discussing with the Stoics, whose philosophy had such a wide ethical significance, and must also have held an important place in the Sceptical School in all metaphysical and philosophical discussions. The definition[5] in the beginning of Sextus' exposition of this Trope Fabricius thinks was taken from Aristotle, of schools, laws, customs, mythical beliefs and dogmatic opinions,[6] and the definition which Diogenes gives of law in his life of Plato[7] is similar. Pappenheim, however, thinks they were taken from the Stoics, perhaps from Chrysippus.[8] The argument is based upon the differences in development of thought, as affecting the standpoint of judgment in philosophy, in morals, and religion, the results of which we find in the widely opposing schools of philosophy, in the variety in religious belief, and in the laws and customs of different countries. Therefore the decisions reached in the world of thought leave us equally in doubt regarding the absolute value of any standards, with those obtained through sense-perception, and the universal conflict of opinion regarding all questions of philosophy and ethics leads us also according to this Trope to the reserving of the opinion.[9] This Trope is the fifth as given by Diogenes, who placed it directly after the first four which relate more especially to human development,[10] while Sextus uses it as the final one, perhaps thinking that an argument based upon the higher powers of man deserves the last place, or is the summation of the other arguments.

[1] *Hyp.* I. 24.

[2] *Hyp.* III. 235.

[3] Diog. IX. 11, 61.

[4] Diog. IX. 11, 83.

[5] *Hyp.* I. 145-147.

[6] Fabricius, Cap. IV. H.

[7] Diog. III. 86.

[8] Pappenheim *Gr. Pyrr. Grundzuege*, p. 50.

[9] *Hyp.* I. 163.

[10] Diog. IX. 11, 83.

Following the exposition of the ten Tropes of the older Sceptics, Sextus gives the five Tropes which he attributes to the "later Sceptics."[1] Sextus nowhere mentions the author of these Tropes. Diogenes, however, attributes them to Agrippa, a man of whom we know nothing except his mention of him. He was evidently one of the followers of Aenesidemus, and a scholar of influence in the Sceptical School, who must have himself had disciples, as Diogenes says, [Greek: hoi peri Agrippan][2] add to these tropes other five tropes, using the plural verb. Another Sceptic, also mentioned by Diogenes, and a man unknown from other sources, named some of his books after Agrippa.[3] Agrippa is not given by Diogenes in the list of the leaders of the Sceptical School, but[4] his influence in the development of the thought of the School must have been great, as the transition from the ten Tropes of the "older Sceptics" to the five attributed to Agrippa is a marked one, and shows the entrance into the school of a logical power before unknown in it. The latter are not a reduction of the Tropes of Aenesidemus, but are written from an entirely different standpoint. The ten Tropes are empirical, and aim to furnish objective proofs of the foundation theories of Pyrrhonism, while the five are rather rules of thought leading to logical proof, and are dialectic in their character. We find this distinction illustrated by the different way in which the Trope of relativity is treated in the two groups. In the first it points to an objective relativity, but with Agrippa to a general subjective logical principle. The originality of the Tropes of Agrippa does not lie in their substance matter, but in their formulation and use in the Sceptical School. These methods of proof were, of course, not new, but were well known to Aristotle, and were used by the Sceptical Academy, and probably also by Timon,[5] while the [Greek: pros ti] goes back at least to Protagoras. The five Tropes are as follows.

(i) The one based upon discord.
(ii) The *regressus in infinitum*.
(iii) Relation.
(iv) The hypothetical.

(v) The *circulus in probando*.

Two of these are taken from the old list, the first and the third, and Sextus says that the five Tropes are intended to supplement the ten Tropes, and to show the audacity of the Dogmatics in a variety of ways.[6] The order of these Tropes is the same with Diogenes as with Sextus, but the definitions of them differ sufficiently to show that the two authors took their material from different sources. According to the first one everything in question is either sensible or intellectual, and in attempting to judge it either in life, practically, or "among philosophers," a position is developed from which it is impossible to reach a conclusion.[7] According to the second, every proof requires another proof, and so on to infinity, and there is no standpoint from which to begin the reasoning.[8] According to the third, all perceptions are relative, as the object is colored by the condition of the judge, and the influence of other things around it.[9] According to the fourth, it is impossible to escape from the *regressus in infinitum* by making a hypothesis the starting point, as the Dogmatics attempt to do.[10] And the fifth, or the *circulus in probando*, arises when that which should be the proof needs to be sustained by the thing to be proved.

[1] *Hyp.* I. 164.

[2] Diog. IX. 11, 88.

[3] Diog. IX. 11, 106.

[4] Diog. IX. 12, 115-116.

[5] Compare Natorp. *Op. cit.* p. 302.

[6] *Hyp.* I. 177.

[7] *Hyp.* I. 165.

[8] *Hyp.* I. 166.

[9] *Hyp.* I. 167.

[10] *Hyp.* I. 168.

Sextus claims that all things can be included in these Tropes, whether sensible or intellectual.[1] For whether, as some say, only the things of sense are true, or as others claim, only those of the understanding, or as still others contend, some things both of sense and understanding are true, a discord must arise that is impossible to be judged, for it cannot be judged by the sensible, nor by the intellectual, for the things of the intellect themselves require a proof; accordingly, the result of all reasoning must be either hypothetical, or fall into the *regressus in infinitum* or the *circulus in probando*.[2] The reference above to some who say that only the things of sense are true, is to Epicurus and Protagoras; to some that only the things of thought are true, to Democritus and Plato; and to those that claimed some of both to be true, to the Stoics and the Peripatetics.[3] The three new Tropes added by Agrippa have nothing to do with sense-perception, but bear entirely upon the possibility of reasoning, as demanded by the science of logic, in contrast to the earlier ones which related almost entirely, with the exception of the tenth, to material objects. Sextus claims that these five Tropes also lead to the suspension of judgment,[4] but their logical result is rather the dogmatic denial of all possibility of knowledge, showing as Hirzel has well demonstrated, far more the influence of the New Academy than the spirit of the Sceptical School.[5] It was the standpoint of the older Sceptics, that although the search for the truth had not yet succeeded, yet they were still seekers, and Sextus claims to be faithful to this old aim of the Pyrrhonists. He calls himself a seeker,[6] and in reproaching the New Academy for affirming that knowledge is impossible, Sextus says, "Moreover, we say that our ideas are equal as regards trustworthiness and untrustworthiness."[7] The ten Tropes claim to establish doubt only in regard to a knowledge of the truth, but the five Tropes of Agrippa aim to logically prove the impossibility of knowledge. It is very strange that Sextus does not see this decided contrast in the attitude of the two sets of Tropes, and expresses his approval of those of Agrippa, and makes more frequent use of the fifth of these, [Greek: ho diallelos], in his subsequent reasoning than of any other argument.[8]

[1] *Hyp.* I. 169.

[2] *Hyp.* I. 170-171.

[3] *Adv. Math.* VIII. 185-186; VIII. 56; VII. 369.

[4] *Hyp.* I. 177.

[5] Hirzel *Op. cit.* p. 131.

[6] *Hyp.* I. 3, 7.

[7] *Hyp.* I. 227.

[8] See Index of Bekker's edition of Sextus' works.

We find here in the Sceptical School, shortly after the time of Aenesidemus, the same tendency to dogmatic teaching that--so far as the dim and shadowy history of the last years of the New Academy can be unravelled, and the separation of Pyrrhonism can be understood, at the time that the Academy passed over into eclecticism--was one of the causes of that separation.

It is true that the Tropes of Agrippa show great progress in the development of thought. They furnish an organisation of the School far superior to what went before, placing the reasoning on the firm basis of the laws of logic, and simplifying the amount of material to be used. In a certain sense Saisset is correct in saying that Agrippa contributed more than any other in completing the organisation of Scepticism,[1] but it is not correct when we consider the true spirit of Scepticism with which the Tropes of Agrippa were not in harmony. It was through the very progress shown in the production of these Tropes that the school finally lost the strength of its position.

Not content with having reduced the number of the Tropes from ten to five, others tried to limit the number still further to two.[2] Sextus gives us no hint of the authorship of the two Tropes. Ritter attributes them to Menodotus and his followers, and Zeller agrees with that opinion,[3] while Saisset thinks that Agrippa was also the author of these,[4] which is a strange theory to propound, as some of the material of the five is repeated in the two, and the same man could certainly not appear as an advocate of five, and at the same time of two Tropes.

[1] Saisset *Op. cit.* p. 237.

[2] *Hyp.* I. 178.

[3] Zeller III. 38; Ritter IV. 277.

[4] Saisset *Op. cit.* p. 231.

The two Tropes are founded on the principle that anything must be known through itself or through something else. It cannot be known through itself, because of the discord existing between all things of the senses and intellect, nor can it be known through something else, as then either the regressus in infinitum *or the* circulus in probando follow.[1] Diogenes Laertius does not refer to these two Tropes.

In regard to all these Tropes of the suspension of judgment, Sextus has well remarked in his introduction to them, that they are included in the eighth, or that of relation.[2]

[1] *Hyp.* I. 178-179.

[2] *Hyp.* I. 39.

The Tropes of Aetiology. The eight Tropes against causality belong chronologically before the five Tropes of Agrippa, in the history of the development of sceptical thought. They have a much closer connection with the spirit of Scepticism than the Tropes of Agrippa, including, as they do, the fundamental thought of Pyrrhonism, *i.e.*, that the phenomena do not reveal the unknown.

The Sceptics did not deny the phenomena, but they denied that the phenomena are signs capable of being interpreted, or of revealing the reality of causes. It is impossible by a research of the signs to find out the unknown, or the explanation of things, as the Stoics and Epicureans claim. The theory of Aenesidemus which lies at the foundation of his eight Tropes against aetiology, is given to us by Photius as follows:[1] "There are no visible signs of the unknown, and those who believe in its existence are the victims of a vain illusion." This statement of Aenesidemus is confirmed by a fuller explanation of it given later on by Sextus.[2] If phenomena are not signs of the unknown there is no causality, and a refutation of causality is a proof of the impossibility of science, as all science is the science of causes, the power of studying causes from effects, or as Sextus calls them, phenomena.

It is very noticeable to any one who reads the refutation of causality by Aenesidemus, as given by Sextus,[3] that there is no reference to the strongest argument of modern Scepticism, since the time of Hume, against causality, namely that the origin of the idea of causality cannot be so accounted for as to justify our relying upon it as a form of cognition.[4]

[1] *Myriob.* 170 B. 12.

[2] *Adv. Math.* VIII. 207.

[3] *Hyp.* I. 180-186.

[4] Ueberweg *Op. cit.* p. 217.

The eight Tropes are directed against the possibility of knowledge of nature, which Aenesidemus contested against in all his Tropes, the ten as well as the eight.[1] They are written from a materialistic standpoint. These Tropes are given with illustrations by Fabricius as follows:

I. Since aetiology in general refers to things that are unseen, it does not give testimony that is incontestable in regard to phenomena. For example, the Pythagoreans explain the distance of the planets by a musical proportion.

II. From many equally plausible reasons which might be given for the same thing, one only is arbitrarily chosen, as some explain the inundation of the Nile by a fall of snow at its source, while there could be other causes, as rain, or wind, or the action of the sun.

III. Things take place in an orderly manner, but the causes presented do not show any order, as for example, the motion of the stars is explained by their mutual pressure, which does not take into account the order that reigns among them.

IV. The unseen things are supposed to take place in the same way as phenomena, as vision is explained in the same way as the appearance of images in a dark room.

V. Most philosophers present theories of aetiology which agree with their own individual hypotheses about the elements, but not with common and accepted ideas, as to explain the world by atoms like Epicurus, by homoeomeriae like Anaxagoras, or by matter and form like Aristotle.

VI. Theories are accepted which agree with individual hypotheses, and others equally probable are passed by, as Aristotle's explanation of comets, that they are a collection of vapors near the earth, because that coincided with his theory of the universe.

VII. Theories of aetiology are presented which conflict not only with individual hypotheses, but also with phenomena, as to admit like Epicurus an inclination or desire of the soul, which was incompatible with the necessity which he advocated.

VIII. The inscrutable is explained by things equally inscrutable, as the rising of sap in plants is explained by the attraction of a sponge for water, a fact contested by some.[2]

[1] *Hyp.* I. 98.

[2] *Hyp.* I. 180-186; Fabricius, Cap. XVII. 180 z.

Diogenes does not mention these Tropes in this form, but he gives a *resume* of the general arguments of the Sceptics against aetiology,[1] which has less in common with the eight Tropes of Aenesidemus, than with the presentation of the subject by Sextus later,[2] when he multiplies his proofs exceedingly to show [Greek: meden einai aition]. Although the Tropes of Aenesidemus have a dialectic rather than an objective character, it would not seem that he made the distinction, which is so prominent with Sextus, between the signs [Greek: hypomnestika] and [Greek: endeiktika],[3] especially as Diogenes sums up his argument on the subject with the general assertion, [Greek: Semeion ouk einai],[4] and proceeds to introduce the logical consequence of the denial of aetiology. The summing up of the Tropes of Aenesidemus is given as follows, in the *Hypotyposes*, by Sextus:--"A cause in harmony with all the sects of philosophy, and with Scepticism, and with phenomena, is perhaps not possible, for the phenomena and the unknown altogether disagree."[5]

It is interesting to remark in connection with the seventh of these Tropes, that Aenesidemus asserts that causality has only a subjective value, which from his materialistic standpoint was an argument against its real existence, and the same argument is used by Kant to prove that causality is a necessary condition of thought.[6]

Chaignet characterises the Tropes of Aenesidemus as false and sophistical,[7] but as Maccoll has well said, they are remarkable for their judicious and strong criticism, and are directed against the false method of observing facts through the light of preconceived opinion.[8] They have, however, a stronger critical side than sceptical, and show the positive tendency of the thought of Aenesidemus.

[1] Diog. IX. 11, 96-98.

[2] *Hyp.* III. 24-28.

[3] *Adv. Math.* VIII. 151.

[4] Diog. IX. 11, 96.

[5] *Hyp.* I. 185.

[6] Compare Maccoll *Op. cit.* p. 77.

[7] Chaignet *Op. cit.* 507.

[8] Maccoll *Op. cit.* p. 88.

CHAPTER IV.

Aenesidemus and the Philosophy of Heraclitus.

A paragraph in the First Book of the **Hypotyposes** which has given rise to much speculation and many different theories, is the comparison which Sextus makes of Scepticism with the philosophy of Heraclitus.[1] In this paragraph the statement is made that Aenesidemus and his followers, [Greek: hoi peri ton Ainesidemon], said that Scepticism is the path to the philosophy of Heraclitus, because the doctrine that contradictory predicates appear to be applicable to the same thing, leads the way to the one that contradictory predicates are in reality applicable to the same thing.[2] [Greek: hoi peri ton Ainesidemon elegon hodon einai ten skeptiken agogen epi ten Herakleiteion philosophian, dioti proegeitai tou tanantia peri to auto hyparchein to tanantia peri to auto phainesthai]. As the Sceptics say that contradictory predicates appear to be applicable to the same thing, the Heraclitans come from this to the more positive doctrine that they are in reality so.[3]

[1] **Hyp.** I. 210.

[2] **Hyp.** I. 210.

[3] **Hyp.** I. 210.

This connection which Aenesidemus is said to have affirmed between Scepticism and the philosophy of Heraclitus is earnestly combated by Sextus, who declares that the fact that contradictory predicates appear to be applicable to the same thing is not a dogma of the Sceptics, but a fact which presents itself to all men, and not to the Sceptics only. No one for instance, whether he be a Sceptic or not, would dare to say that honey does not taste sweet to those in health, and bitter to those who have the jaundice, so that Heraclitus begins from a preconception common to all men, as to us also, and perhaps to the other schools of philosophy as well.[1] As the statement concerning the appearance of contradictory predicates in regard to the same thing is not an exclusively sceptical one, then Scepticism is no more a path to the philosophy of Heraclitus than to other schools of philosophy, or to life, as all use common subject matter. "But we are afraid that the Sceptical School not only does not help towards the knowledge of the philosophy of Heraclitus, but even hinders that result. Since the Sceptic accuses Heraclitus of having rashly dogmatised, presenting on the one hand the doctrine of 'conflagration' and on the other that 'contradictory predicates are in reality applicable to the same thing.'"[2] "It is absurd, then, to say that this conflicting school is a path to the sect with which it conflicts. It is therefore absurd to say that the Sceptical School is a path to the philosophy of Heraclitus."[3]

[1] *Hyp.* I. 211.

[2] *Hyp.* I. 212.

[3] *Hyp.* I. 212.

This is not the only place in the writings of Sextus which states that Aenesidemus at some time of his life was an advocate of the doctrines of Heraclitus. In no instance, however, where

Sextus refers to this remarkable fact, does he offer any explanation of it, or express any bitterness against Aenesidemus, whom he always speaks of with respect as a leader of the Sceptical School. We are thus furnished with one of the most difficult problems of ancient Scepticism, the problem of reconciling the apparent advocacy of Aenesidemus of the teachings of Heraclitus with his position in the Sceptical School.

A comparison with each other of the references made by Sextus and other writers to the teachings of Aenesidemus, and a consideration of the result, gives us two pictures of Aenesidemus which conflict most decidedly with each other. We have on the one hand, the man who was the first to give Pyrrhonism a position as an influential school, and the first to collect and present to the world the results of preceding Sceptical thought. He was the compiler of the ten Tropes of [Greek: epoche], and perhaps in part their author, and the author of the eight Tropes against aetiology.[1] He develops his Scepticism from the standpoint that neither the senses nor the intellect can give us any certain knowledge of reality.[2] He denied the possibility of studying phenomena as signs of the unknown.[3] He denied all possibility of truth, and the reality of motion, origin and decay. There was according to his teaching no pleasure or happiness, and no wisdom or supreme good. He denied the possibility of finding out the nature of things, or of proving the existence of the gods, and finally he declared that no ethical aim is possible.

[1] *Hyp.* I. 180.

[2] Photius 170, B. 12.

[3] ***Adv. Math.*** VIII. 40.

The picture on the other hand, presented to us by Sextus and Tertullian, is that of a man with a system of beliefs and dogmas, which lead, he says, to the philosophy of Heraclitus. In strange contradiction to his assertion of the impossibility of all knowledge, he advocates a theory that the original substance is air,[1] which is most certainly a dogma, although indeed a deviation from the teachings of Heraclitus, of which Sextus seemed unconscious, as he says, [Greek: to te on kata ton Herakleiton aer estin, hos physin ho Ainesidemos]. Aenesidemus dogmatised also regarding number and time and unity of the original world-stuff.[2] He seems to have dogmatised further about motion,[3] and about the soul.[4]

If Sextus' language is taken according to its apparent meaning, we find ourselves here in the presence of a system of beliefs which would be naturally held by a follower of the Stoic-Heraclitan physics,[5] and absolutely inexplicable from the standpoint of a man who advocated so radical a Scepticism as Aenesidemus. Sextus in the passage that we first quoted,[6] expresses great indignation against the idea that Scepticism could form the path to the philosophy of Heraclitus, but he does not express surprise or indignation against Aenesidemus personally, or offer any explanation of the apparent contradiction; and while his writings abound in references to him as a respected leader of the Sceptical School, he sometimes seems to include him with the Dogmatics, mentioning him with the [Greek: dogmatikon philosophon].[7] In fact, the task of presenting any consistent history of the development of thought through which Aenesidemus passed is such a puzzling one, that Brochard brilliantly remarks that possibly the best attitude to take towards it would be to follow the advice of Aenesidemus himself, and suspend one's judgment altogether regarding it. Is it possible to suppose that so sharp and subtle a thinker as Aenesidemus held at the same time such opposing opinions?

[1] *Adv. Math.* X. 233.

[2] *Adv. Math.* IX. 337; X. 216.

[3] *Adv. Math.* X. 38.

[4] *Adv. Math.* VII. 349.

[5] Compare Zeller *Op. cit.* III. p. 33.

[6] *Hyp.* I. 210-212.

[7] *Adv. Math.* VIII. 8; X. 215.

The conjecture that he was first a Heraclitan Stoic, and later a Sceptic, which might be possible, does not offer any explanation of Sextus' statement, that he regarded Scepticism as a path to the philosophy of Heraclitus. Nor would it be logical to think that after establishing the Sceptical School in renewed influence and power, he reverted to the Heraclitan theories as they were modified by the Stoics. These same theories were the cause of his separation from the Academy, for his chief accusation against the Academy was that it was adopting the dogmatism of the Stoics.[1] The matter is complicated by the fact that Tertullian also attributes to Aenesidemus anthropological and physical teachings that agree with the Stoical Heraclitan doctrines. It is not strange that in view of these contradictory assertions in regard to the same man, some have suggested the possibility that they referred to two different men of the same name, a supposition, however, that no one has been able to authoritatively vindicate.

Let us consider briefly some of the explanations which have been attempted of the apparent heresy of Aenesidemus towards the Sceptical School. We will begin with the most ingenious, that of Pappenheim.[2]

Pappenheim claims that Sextus was not referring to Aenesidemus himself in these statements which he joins with his name. In the most important of these, the one quoted from the *Hypotyposes*,[3] which represents Aenesidemus as claiming that Scepticism is the path to the philosophy of Heraclitus, the expression used is [Greek: hoi peri ton Ainesidemon], and in many of the other places where Sextus refers to the dogmatic statements of Aenesidemus, the expression is either [Greek: hoi peri ton Ainesidemon], or [Greek: Ainesidemos kath' Herakleiton], while when Sextus quotes Aenesidemus to sustain Scepticism, he uses his name alone.

[1] Compare Zeller *Op. cit.* III. p. 16.

[2] Die angebliche Heraclitismus des Skeptikers Ainesidemos, Berlin 1889.

[3] *Hyp.* I. 210-212.

Pappenheim thinks that Sextus' conflict was not with the dead Aenesidemus, who had lived two centuries before him, but with his own contemporaries. He also seeks to prove that Sextus could not have gained his knowledge of these sayings of Aenesidemus from any of Aenesidemus' own writings, as neither by the ancients, nor by later writers, was any book spoken of which could well have contained them. Neither Aristocles nor Diogenes mentions any such book.

Pappenheim also makes much of the argument that Sextus in no instance seems conscious of inconsistency on the part of Aenesidemus, even when most earnestly combating his alleged teachings, but in referring to him personally he always speaks of him with great respect.

Pappenheim suggests, accordingly, that the polemic of Sextus was against contemporaries, those who accepted the philosophy of Heraclitus in consequence of, or in some connection with, the teachings of Aenesidemus. He entirely ignores the fact that there is no trace of any such school or sect in history, calling themselves followers of "Aenesidemus according to Heraclitus," but still thinks it possible that such a movement existed in Alexandria at the time of Sextus, where so many different sects were found. Sextus use Aenesidemus' name in four different ways:--alone, [Greek: hoi peri ton Ainesidemon], [Greek: Ainesidemos kath' Herakleiton], and in one instance [Greek: hoi peri ton Ainesidemon kath' Herakleiton].[1]

[1] ***Adv. Math.*** VIII. 8.

Pappenheim advances the theory that some of these contemporaries against whom Sextus directed his arguments had written a book entitled [Greek: Ainesidemos kath' Herakleiton], to prove the harmony between Aenesidemus and Heraclitus, and that it was from this book that Sextus quoted the dogmatic statements which he introduced with that formula. He claims, further, that the passage quoted from *Hypotyposes I.* even, is directed against contemporaries, who founded their system of proofs of the harmony between Aenesidemus and Heraclitus on the connection of the celebrated formula which was such a favourite with the Sceptics: "Contrary predicates appear to apply to the same thing," with the apparent deduction from this, that "Contrary predicates in reality apply to the same thing." Sextus wishes, according to Pappenheim, to prove to these contemporaries that they had misunderstood Aenesidemus, and Sextus does not report Aenesidemus to be a Dogmatic, nor to have taught the doctrines of Heraclitus; neither has he misunderstood Aenesidemus, nor consequently misrepresented him; but on the contrary, these dogmatic quotations have nothing to do with Aenesidemus, but refer altogether to contemporaries who pretended to be Sceptics while they accepted the teachings of Heraclitus. Sextus naturally warmly combats this tendency, as he wishes to preserve Pyrrhonism pure.

Brochard advocates a change of opinion on the part of Aenesidemus as an explanation of the difficulty in question.[1] He starts from the supposition, the reasonableness of which we shall consider later, that Aenesidemus had passed through one change of opinion already when he severed his connection with the New Academy; and to the two phases of his life, which such a change has already made us familiar with, he adds a third. Aenesidemus would not be the first who has accepted different beliefs at different periods of his life, and Brochard claims that such a development in the opinions of Aenesidemus is logical. He does not accuse Aenesidemus of having, as might seem from the perusal of Sextus, suddenly changed his basis, but rather of having gradually come to accept much in the teachings of Heraclitus. Aenesidemus modifies his Scepticism only to the extent of pretending to know something of absolute reality. The Sceptic says, "Contradictory predicates are apparently applicable to the same thing," and Aenesidemus accepts the Heraclitan result--"Contradictory predicates are in reality applicable to the same thing." From Sextus' report, Aenesidemus would seem to have renounced his position as a Sceptic in saying that Scepticism is the path to the philosophy of Heraclitus. He does not, however, renounce Scepticism, but he finds it incomplete. In deliberating concerning the appearance of contradictory predicates in regard to the same object, he would naturally ask, "Whence come these contradictory appearances?" After having doubted all things, he wished to know wherefore he doubts. The system of Heraclitus offers a solution, and he accepts it. Contradictory predicates produce equilibrium in the soul because they are an expression of reality.

[1] Brochard *Op. cit.* 272.

As a Sceptic he claims that knowledge is impossible, and he does not find that the statement of Heraclitus disproves this, but rather that it supports his theory. He had denied the existence of science. He still does so, but now he knows why he denies it. Brochard asks why it is any more impossible that Aenesidemus should have been a follower of Heraclitus than that Protagoras was so, as Protagoras was after all a Sceptic. In conclusion, Brochard claims that the dogmatic theories attributed to Aenesidemus relate to the doctrine of the truth of contradictory predicates, which seemed to him a logical explanation of the foundation theories of Scepticism. It is right to call him a Sceptic, for he was so, and that sincerely; and he deserves his rank as one of the chiefs of the Sceptical School.

Coming now to the opinion of Zeller,[1] we find that he advocates a misconception of Aenesidemus on the part of Sextus. The whole difficulty is removed, Zeller thinks, by the simple fact that Sextus had not understood Aenesidemus; and as Tertullian and Sextus agree in this misconception of the views

of Aenesidemus, they must have been misled by consulting a
common author in regard to Aenesidemus, who confused what
Aenesidemus said of Heraclitus with his own opinion. Zeller
maintains that the expression so often repeated by
Sextus--[Greek: Ainesidemos kath' Herakleiton]--shows that some
one of Aenesidemus' books contained a report of Heraclitus'
doctrines, as Aenesidemus was in the habit of quoting as many
authorities as possible to sustain his Scepticism. To justify
his quotations from Heraclitus, he had possibly given a short
abstract of Heraclitus' teachings; and the misconception
advocated by Zeller and found both in Tertullian and Sextus,
refers rather to the spirit than to the words quoted from
Aenesidemus, and is a misconception due to some earlier author,
who had given a false impression of the meaning of Aenesidemus
in quoting what Aenesidemus wrote about Heraclitus. That is to
say, Heraclitus was classed by Aenesidemus only among those who
prepared the way for Scepticism, just as Diogenes[2] mentions
many philosophers in that way; and that Soranus[3] and Sextus
both had the same misunderstanding can only be explained by a
mistake on the part of the authority whom they consulted.

[1] Zeller *Op. cit.* III, pp. 31-35; Grundriss der
Geschichte der Griechischen Phil. p. 263.

[2] Diog. Laert. IX. 11, 71-74.

[3] Tertullian.

This explanation, however, makes Sextus a very stupid man.
Aenesidemus' books were well known, and Sextus would most
certainly take the trouble to read them. His reputation as an
historian would not sustain such an accusation, as Diogenes
calls his books [Greek: ta deka ton skeptikon kai alla

kallista].[1] Furthermore, that Sextus used Aenesidemus' own books we know from the direct quotation from them in regard to Plato,[2] which he combines with the ideas of Menodotus[3] and his own.

[1] Diog. IX. 12, 116.

[2] *Hyp.* I. 222.

[3] Following the Greek of Bekker.

Sextus' references to Aenesidemus in connection with Heraclitus are very numerous, and it is absurd to suppose that he would have trusted entirely to some one who reported him for authority on such a subject. Even were it possible that Sextus did not refer directly to the works of Aenesidemus, which we do not admit, even then, there had been many writers in the Sceptical School since the time of Aenesidemus, and they certainly could not all have misrepresented him. We must remember that Sextus was at the head of the School, and had access to all of its literature. His honor would not allow of such a mistake, and if he had indeed made it, his contemporaries must surely have discovered it before Diogenes characterised his books as [Greek: kallista]. Whatever may be said against the accuracy of Sextus as a general historian of philosophy, especially in regard to the older schools, he cannot certainly be accused of ignorance respecting the school of which he was at that time the head.

The opinion of Ritter on this subject is that Aenesidemus must have been a Dogmatic.[1] Saisset contends[2] that Aenesidemus really passed from the philosophy of Heraclitus to that of Pyrrho, and made the statement that Scepticism is the path to the philosophy of Heraclitus to defend his change of view, although in his case the change had been just the opposite to the one he defends. Saisset propounds as a law in the history of philosophy a fact which he claims to be true, that Scepticism always follows sensationalism, for which he gives two examples, Pyrrho, who was first a disciple of Democritus, and Hume, who was a disciple of Locke It is not necessary to discuss the absurdity of such a law, which someone has well remarked would involve an *a priori* construction of history. There is no apparent reason for Saisset's conjecture in regard to Aenesidemus, for it is exactly the opposite of what Sextus has reported. Strange to say, Saisset himself remarks in another place that we owe religious respect to any text, and that it should be the first law of criticism to render this.[3] Such respect to the text of Sextus, as he himself advocates, puts Saisset's explanation of the subject under discussion out of the question.

[1] Ritter, *Op. cit.* p. 280. Book IV.

[2] Saisset, *Op. cit.* p. 206.

[3] Saisset *Op. cit.* p. 206.

Hirzel and Natorp do not find such a marked contradiction in the two views presented of the theories of Aenesidemus, nor do they think that Sextus has misrepresented them. They rather maintain, that in declaring the coexistence of contradictory predicates regarding the same object, Aenesidemus does not cease to be a Sceptic, for he did not believe that the predicates are applicable in a dogmatic sense of the word, but are only applicable in appearance, that is, applicable to phenomena. The Heraclitism of Aenesidemus would be then only in appearance, as he understood the statement, that "Contradictory predicates are in reality applicable to the same thing," only in the phenomenal sense.[1] Hirzel says in addition, that contradictory predicates are in reality applicable to those phenomena which are the same for all, and consequently true, for Aenesidemus considered those phenomena true that are the same for all.[2] As Protagoras, the disciple of Heraclitus, declared the relative character of sensations, that things exist only for us, and that their nature depends on our perception of them; so, in the phenomenal sense, Aenesidemus accepts the apparent fact that contradictory predicates in reality apply to the same thing.

[1] Natorp *Op. cit.* 115, 122.

[2] **Adv. Math.** VIII. 8; Hirzel *Op. cit.* p. 95.

This explanation entirely overlooks the fact that we have to do with the word [Greek: huparchein], in the statement that contradictory predicates in reality apply to the same thing; while in the passage quoted where Aenesidemus declares common phenomena to be true ones, we have the word [Greek: alethe], so that this explanation of the difficulty would advocate a very strange use of the word [Greek: huparchein].

All of these different views of the possible solution of this perplexing problem are worthy of respect, as the opinion of men who have given much thought to this and other closely Belated subjects. While we may not altogether agree with any one of them, they nevertheless furnish many suggestions, which are very valuable in helping to construct a theory on the subject that shall satisfactorily explain the difficulties, and present a consistent view of the attitude of Aenesidemus.

First, in regard to the Greek expression [Greek: hoi peri] in connection with proper names, upon which Pappenheim bases so much of his argument. All Greek scholars would agree that the expression does not apply usually only to the disciples of any teacher, but [Greek: hoi peri ton Ainesidemon], for instance, includes Aenesidemus with his followers, and is literally translated, "Aenesidemus and his followers." It is noticeable, however, in the writings of Sextus that he uses the expression [Greek: hoi peri] often for the name of the founder of a school alone, as Pappenheim himself admits.[1] We find examples of this in the mention of Plato and Democritus and Arcesilaus, as [Greek: hoi peri ton Platona kai Demokriton][2] and [Greek: hoi peri ton Arkesilaon],[3] and accordingly we have no right to infer that his use of the name Aenesidemus in this way has an exceptional significance. It may mean Aenesidemus alone, or it may signify Aenesidemus in connection with his followers.

[1] Pappenheim *Op. cit.* p. 21.

[2] *Adv. Math.* VIII. 6.

[3] *Adv. Math.* VII. 150.

In reply to Zeller's position, that Sextus and Tertullian have misunderstood Aenesidemus, and quote from some common author who misrepresents him, we would admit that such a misunderstanding might be possible where Sextus gives long explanations of Heraclitus' teachings, beginning with quoting Aenesidemus, and continuing in such a way that it is not always possible to distinguish just the part that is attributed to Aenesidemus; but such a misunderstanding certainly cannot be asserted in regard to the direct statement that Aenesidemus regarded Scepticism as the path to the philosophy of Heraclitus, for the reasons previously given. Neither would we agree with Brochard, whose solution of the difficulty is on the whole the most logical, *i.e.*, that Aenesidemus had necessarily already passed through two phases of philosophical belief. It is possible to admit a gradual evolution of thought in Aenesidemus without supposing in either case a change of basis. His withdrawal from the Academy is an argument against, rather than in favor of a change on his part, and was caused by the well-known change in the attitude of the Academy.

Many of the teachings of the Sceptical School were taken directly from the Academy, belonging to those doctrines advocated in the Academy before the eclectic dogmatic tendency introduced by Antiochus. In fact, Sextus himself claims a close relation between the Middle Academy and Pyrrhonism.[1] Aenesidemus, although he was a Sceptic, belonged to the Academy, and on leaving it became, as it were, a pioneer in Pyrrhonism, and cannot be judged in the same way as we should judge a Sceptic of Sextus' time.

It seems a self-evident fact that during the two centuries which elapsed between the time of Aenesidemus and Sextus, the standpoint of judgment in the Sceptical School had greatly changed. An example illustrating this change we find in a comparison of the presentation of Scepticism by Diogenes with that of Sextus. The author Whom Diogenes follows, probably one of the Sceptical writers, considers Xenophanes, Zeno, and Democritus, Sceptics, and also Plato,[2] while Sextus, in regard to all of these men, opposes the idea that they were Sceptics.[3] Diogenes also calls Heraclitus a Sceptic, and even Homer,[4] and quotes sceptical sayings from the Seven Wise Men;[5] he includes in the list of Sceptics, Archilochus, Euripides, Empedocles, and Hippocrates,[6] and, furthermore, says that Theodosius, probably one of the younger Sceptics, objected to the name 'Pyrrhonean' on the ground that Pyrrho was not the first Sceptic.[7]

[1] *Hyp.* I. 232.

[2] Diog. IX. 11, 17-72.

[3] *Hyp.* I. 213-214; I. 223-225.

[4] Diog. IX. 11, 71.

[5] Diog. IX. 11, 71.

[6] Diog. IX. 11, 71-73.

[7] Diog. IX. 11. 70.

We have given the testimony from many sources to the effect that before the time of Sextus the Empirical School of Medicine was considered identical with Scepticism, although not so by Sextus himself. From all of these things we may infer a narrowing of the limits of Pyrrhonism in the time of Sextus.

Let us accept with Brochard the development of thought seen in Aenesidemus from the beginning to the end of his career, without agreeing with him that Aenesidemus ever consciously changed his basis. He was a Sceptic in the Academy. He left the Academy on that account, and he remained a Sceptic to the end, in so far as a man can be a Sceptic, and take the positive stand that Aenesidemus did.

Two things might account for his apparent dogmatism--

(i) The eclectic spirit of his time.

(ii) The psychological effect upon himself of this careful systemisation of the Sceptical teachings.

Let us consider the first of these causes. Aenesidemus, although not the first of the later Sceptics, was apparently the first to separate himself from the Academy. He was the founder of a new movement, the attempt to revive the older Scepticism as taught by Pyrrho and Timon, and separate it from the dogmatic teachings of the Stoics which were so greatly affecting the Scepticism of the New Academy. It was the spirit of his time to seek to sustain all philosophical teaching by the authority of as many as possible of the older philosophers, and he could hardly escape the tendency which his training in the Academy had unconsciously given him. Therefore we find him trying to prove that the philosophy of Heraclitus follows from Scepticism. It is not necessary either to explain the matter, as both Hirzel and Natorp so ingeniously attempt to do, by claiming that the truth of contradictory predicates which Aenesidemus accepted from Heraclitus referred only to phenomena. The history of philosophy gives us abundant proof of the impossibility of absolute Scepticism, and Aenesidemus furnishes us with one example of many of this impossibility, and of the dogmatism that must exist in connection with all thought. In the case of Aenesidemus, who evidently gave the best efforts of his life to establish the Sceptical School, the dogmatism was probably unconscious. That he remained to the end a Sceptic is shown by the fact that he was known as such to posterity. Nowhere do we find a change of basis referred to in regard to him, and Sextus, in refuting the mistakes which he attributes to Aenesidemus, does it, as it were, to point out something of which Aenesidemus had been unconscious.

Let us consider here the second cause of Aenesidemus' Dogmatism, the psychological effect upon himself of formulating Sceptical beliefs. The work that he did for the Sceptical School was a positive one. It occupied years of his life, and stamped itself upon his mental development. In formulating Scepticism, and in advocating it against the many enemies of the School, and amidst all the excitement of the disruption from the Academy, and of establishing a new School, it was inevitable that his mind should take a dogmatic tendency. He remained a Sceptic as he had always been, but must have grown dogmatic in his attitude towards the Sceptical formulae, and was thus able to adopt some of the teachings of Heraclitus, unconscious of their inconsistency.

Where should we find a modern writer who is consistent in all his statements? Could we read the works of Aenesidemus, we might better understand the connection between the apparently contradictory ideas in his teaching, but the inconsistencies in statement would probably remain. It is necessary to remember the position of Aenesidemus in breaking away from the Academy and in founding a new school, the full significance of which he could not foresee. There must necessarily be some crudeness in pioneer work, and some failure to see the bearing of all its parts, and a compiler like Sextus could point out the inconsistencies which the two centuries since the time of Aenesidemus had made plain. Aenesidemus was too positive a character to admit of absolute Sceptical consistency. He was nevertheless the greatest thinker the Sceptical School had known since the age of Pyrrho, its founder. In claiming a union between Pyrrhonism and the philosophy of Heraclitus, he recognised also the pre-Socratic tendency of the Sceptical School. The name of Socrates was all powerful in the Academy, but Aenesidemus comprehended the fact that the true spirit of Pyrrhonism was of earlier origin than the Academic Scepsis.

CHAPTER V.

Critical Examination of Pyrrhonism.

The distinct philosophical movement of which Pyrrho was the author bore his name for five centuries after his death. It had an acknowledged existence as a philosophical tendency, if indeed not a sect, for a great part of that time. Yet, when we carefully analyse the relation of Pyrrhonism, as presented to us by Sextus, to the teachings of Pyrrho himself, in so far as they can be known, we find many things in Pyrrhonism for which Pyrrho was not responsible.

The foundation elements of the movement, the spirit of Empirical doubt that lay underneath and caused its development in certain directions rather than others, are due to Pyrrho. The methods of the school, however, were very foreign to anything found in the life or teachings of Pyrrho. Pyrrho was eminently a moralist. He was also to a great degree an ascetic, and he lived his philosophy, giving it thus a positive side wanting in the Pyrrhonism presented to us by Sextus. Timon represents him as desiring to escape from the tedious philosophical discussions of his time--

[Greek:
o geron o Purrhon, pos e pothen ekdusin heures

latreies doxon te kenophrosunes te sophiston;]

and again he speaks of his modest and tranquil life--

[Greek:
touto moi, o Purrhon, himeiretai etor akousai
pos pot' aner et' ageis panta meth' hesuchies
mounos d'anthropoisi theou tropon hegemoneueis
..... pheista meth' hesuchies
aiei aphrontistos kai akinetos kata tauta
me prosech' indalmois hedulogou sophies.][1]

Pyrrho wished more than anything else to live in peace, and his dislike of the Sophists[2] may well have made him try to avoid dialectic; while, on the contrary, in the Pyrrhonean School of later times discussion was one of the principal methods of contest, at least after the time of Agrippa. Pyrrhonism seems to have been originally a theory of life, like the philosophy of Socrates, to whom Pyrrho is often compared,[3] and Pyrrho, like Socrates, lived his philosophy. Our knowledge of Pyrrho is gained from Aristocles, Sextus Empiricus, and Diogenes, and from the Academic traditions given by Cicero. Diogenes gives us details of his life which he attributes to Antigonus of Carystius, who lived about the time of Pyrrho.[4] Pyrrho was a disciple and admirer of Democritus,[5] some of whose teachings bore a lasting influence over the subsequent development of Pyrrhonism. He accompanied Alexander the Great to India, where he remained as a member of his suite for some time, and the philosophical ideas of India were not without influence on his teachings. Oriental philosophy was not unknown in Greece long before the time of Pyrrho, but his personal contact with the Magi and the Gymnosophists of the far East, apparently impressed upon his mind teachings for which he was not unprepared by his previous study and natural disposition. In his indifference to worldly goods we find a strong trace of the Buddhistic teaching regarding the vanity of human life. He showed also a similar hopelessness in regard to the possibility of finding a satisfactory philosophy, or absolute truth. He evidently returned from India with the conviction that truth was not to be attained.[6]

[1] Diog. IX. 11, 65. Given from Mullach's edition of Timon by Brochard, *Pyrrhon et le Scepticism primitive*, p. 525.

[2] Diog. IX. 11, 69.

[3] Lewes *Op. cit.* p. 460.

[4] Diog. IX. 11, 62.

[5] Diog. IX. 11, 67.

[6] Compare Maccoll *Op. cit.*

After the death of Alexander and Pyrrho's return to Greece, he lived quietly with his sister at Elis, and Diogenes says that he was consistent in his life, asserting and denying nothing, but in everything withholding his opinion, as nothing in itself is good or shameful, just or unjust.[1] He was not a victim of false pride, but sold animals in the market place, and, if necessary, washed the utensils himself.[2] He lived in equality of spirit, and practised his teachings with serenity. If one went out while he was talking he paid no attention, but went calmly on with his remarks.[3] He liked to live alone, and to travel alone, and on one occasion, being knocked about in a vessel by a storm at sea, he did not lose his imperturbability, but pointed to a swine calmly eating on board, and said that the wise man should have as much calmness of soul as that. He endured difficult surgical operations with indifference,[4] and when his friend Anaxarchus was once unfortunate enough to fall into a morass, he went calmly by without stopping to help him, for which consistency of conduct Anaxarchus afterwards praised him. There are two instances given by Diogenes when he lost control of himself; once in getting angry with his sister, and once in trying to save himself when chased by a dog. When accused of inconsistency, he said it was difficult to entirely give up one's humanity.[5] He was greatly venerated by the people among whom he lived, who made him high priest, and on his account exempted all philosophers from taxation,[6] and after his death erected a statue to his memory. These facts testify to his moral character, and also to fulfil the functions of high priest a certain amount of dogmatism must have been necessary.

[1] Diog. IX. 11, 61, 62.

[2] Diog. IX. 11, 66.

[3] Diog. IX. 11, 63.

[4] Diog. IX. 11, 67.

[5] Diog. IX. 11, 66.

[6] Diog. IX. 11, 64.

According to Diogenes, "We cannot know," said Pyrrho, "what things are in themselves, either by sensation or by judgment, and, as we cannot distinguish the true from the false, therefore we should live impassively, and without an opinion." The term [Greek: epoche], so characteristic of Pyrrhonism, goes back, according to Diogenes, to the time of Pyrrho.[1] Nothing is, in itself, one thing more than another, but all experience is related to phenomena, and no knowledge is possible through the senses.[2] Pyrrho's aim was [Greek: ataraxia] and his life furnished a marked example of the spirit of indifference, for which the expression [Greek: apatheia] is better suited than the later one, [Greek: ataraxia]. The description of his life with his sister confirms this, where the term [Greek: adiaphoria] is used to describe his conduct.[3] He founded his Scepticism on the equivalence of opposing arguments.[4]

[1] Diog. IX. 11, 61.

[2] Diog. IX. 11, 61-62.

[3] Diog. IX. 11. 66.

[4] Diog. IX. 11. 106.

The picture given of Pyrrho by Cicero is entirely different from that of Diogenes, and contrasts decidedly with it.[1] Cicero knows Pyrrho as a severe moralist, not as a Sceptic. Both authors attribute to Pyrrho the doctrine of indifference and apathy, but, according to Cicero, Pyrrho taught of virtue, honesty, and the ***summum bonum***, while Diogenes plainly tells us that he considered nothing as good in itself, "and of all things nothing as true."[2] Cicero does not once allude to Pyrrhonean doubt. We see on the one hand, in Cicero's idea of Pyrrho, the influence of the Academy, perhaps even of Antiochus himself,[3] which probably colored the representations given of Pyrrho; but, on the other hand, there is much in Diogenes' account of

Pyrrho's life and teachings, and in the writings of Timon, which shows us the positive side of Pyrrho. Pyrrho, in denying the possibility of all knowledge, made that rather a motive for indifference in the relations of life, than the foundation thought of a philosophical system. His teaching has a decided ethical side, showing in that respect the strong influence of Democritus over him, who, like Pyrrho, made happiness to consist in a state of feeling.[4] The one motive of all of Pyrrho's teaching is a positive one, the desire for happiness.

[1] *De orat.* III, 62.

[2] Diog. IX. 11, 61.

[3] Compare Natorp *Op. cit.* p. 71.

[4] Zeller *Grundriss der Griechischen Phil.* p. 70.

The essence of Pyrrhonism as given by Timon is as follows:[1] Man desires to be happy. To realise his desire he must consider three things:

(i) What is the nature of things?

(ii) How should man conduct himself in relation to them?

(iii) What is the result to him of this relation?

The nature of things is unknown. Our relation to them must be one of suspension of judgment, without activity, desire, or belief,--that is, an entirely negative relation. The result is that state of having no opinion, called [Greek: epoche], which is followed in turn by [Greek: ataraxia].

[1] Aristocles *ap. Eusebium Praep. Ev.* XIV. 18.

[1]The problem of philosophy is here proposed very nearly in the terms of Kant, but not with the positive motive, like that of the great philosopher of Germany, of evolving a system to present the truth. Yet the importance of these questions shows the originality of Pyrrho. The earnestness of Pyrrho is further shown by an example given by Diogenes. Once on being found talking to himself alone, he said, when asked the reason, that he was meditating how to become a good man ([Greek: chrestos]),[2] thus showing an entirely different spirit from anything found in Sextus' books. The explanation of his life and teachings is to be found largely in his own disposition. Such an attitude of indifference must belong to a placid nature, and cannot be entirely the result of a philosophical system, and, while it can be aimed at, it can never be perfectly imitated. One of his disciples recognised this, and said that it was necessary to have the disposition of Pyrrho in order to hold his doctrines.[3] Diogenes tells us that he was the first to advance any formulae of Scepticism,[4] but they must have been very elementary, as Pyrrho himself wrote nothing. We find no trace of formulated Tropes in Pyrrho's teachings, yet it is probable that he indicated some of the contradictions in sensation, and possibly the Tropes in some rudimentary form. Of the large number of sceptical formulae, or [Greek: phonai], the three which seem to have the oldest connection with Scepticism are the [Greek: antilogia], the [Greek: ouden horizo], and the [Greek: ou mallon].[5] We know from Diogenes that Protagoras is the authority for saying that in regard to everything there are two opposing arguments.[6] The saying "to determine nothing" is quoted from Timon's *Python* by Diogenes,[7] and the other two

mentioned are also attributed to him by Aristocles.[8] We have also in the [Greek: ou mallon] a direct connection with Democritus, although the difference in the meaning which he attributed to it is shown by Sextus.[9] So while the expression is the same, the explanation of it given by Pyrrho must have been different. It would seem probable that Pyrrho used all of these three sayings, from the account of Diogenes, and that even then they gave rise to the accusation of the Dogmatics, that simply by possessing such sayings the Sceptics dogmatised,[10] for the refutation of this used by Sextus occurs in the old account of the sayings, namely, that these formulae include also themselves in the meaning, as a cathartic removes itself together with other harmful objects.[11]

[1] Compare Maccoll *Op. cit.* p. 21.

[2] Diog. IX. 11, 64.

[3] Diog. IX. 11, 70, 64.

[4] Diog. IX. 11, 69; IX. 11, 61.

[5] *Hyp.* I. 202; Diog. IX. 8, 51; *Photius* Bekker's ed. 280 H.

[6] *Photius* Bekker's ed. 280 H.

[7] *Hyp.* I. 197; Diog. IX. 11, 76.

[8] *Aristocles ap. Eusebium, Praep. Ev.* XIV. 18.

[9] *Hyp.* I. 213.

[10] Diog. IX. 11, 68-76.

[11] Diog. IX. 11, 76; *Hyp.* I. 206.

In comparing the later Pyrrhonism with the teachings of Pyrrho, we would sharply contrast the moral attitude of the two. With Pyrrho equilibrium of soul was a means to be applied to his positive theory of life; with the later Pyrrhoneans it was the end to be attained. We would attribute, however, the empirical tendency shown during the whole history of Pyrrhonism to Pyrrho as its originator. He was an empirical philosopher, and the result of his influence in this respect, as seen in the subsequent development of the school, stands in marked contrast to the dialectic spirit of the Academic Scepsis. The empiricism of the school is shown in its scientific lore, in the fact that so many of the Sceptics were physicians, and in the character of the ten Tropes of [Greek: epoche]. We may safely affirm that the foundation principles of Pyrrhonism are due to Pyrrho, and the originality which gave the school its power. The elaborated arguments, however, and the details of its formulae belong to later times.

Coming now to the relation of Pyrrhonism to the Academy, the connection between the two is difficult to exactly determine, between the time of Pyrrho and that of Aenesidemus. Scepticism in the Academy was, however, never absolutely identical with Pyrrhonism, although at certain periods of the history of the Academy the difference was slight. We can trace throughout the evolution of doubt, as shown to us in Pyrrhonism, and in Academic Scepticism, the different results which followed the difference in origin of the two movements, and these differences followed according to general laws of development of thought. Arcesilaus, who introduced doubt into the Academy, claimed to return to the dialectic of Socrates, and suppressing the lectures,[1] which were the method of teaching in the later schools of philosophy, introduced discussions instead, as being more decidedly a Socratic method. Although, according to Sextus, he was the one leader of the Academy whose Scepticism most nearly approached that of Pyrrhonism,[2] yet underneath his whole teaching lay that dialectic principle so thoroughly in opposition to the empiricism of Pyrrho. The belief of Socrates and Plato in the existence of absolute truth never entirely lost its influence over the Academy, but was like a hidden germ, destined to reappear after Scepticism had passed away. It finally led the Academy back to Dogmatism, and prepared the way for the Eclecticism with which it disappeared from history.

[1] Compare Maccoll *Op. cit.* p. 36.

[2] *Hyp*. I. 232.

The history of Pyrrhonism and that of Academic Scepticism were for a time contemporaneous. The immediate follower of Pyrrho, Timon, called by Sextus the "prophet of Pyrrho,"[1] was a contemporary of Arcesilaus. That he did not consider the Scepticism of the Academy identical with Pyrrhonism is proved from the fact that he did not himself join the Academy, but was, on the contrary, far from doing so. That he regarded Arcesilaus as a Dogmatic is evident from his writings.[2] One day, on seeing the chief of the Academy approaching, he cried out, "What are you doing here among us who are free?"[3] After the death of Timon, the Pyrrhonean School had no representative till the time of Ptolemy of Cyrene,[4] and Greek Scepticism was represented by the Academy. That Pyrrho had a strong influence over Arcesilaus, the founder of the Middle Academy, is evident[5]; but there was also never a time when the Academy entirely broke away from all the teachings of Plato, even in their deepest doubt.[6] It is true that Arcesilaus removed, nominally as well as in spirit, some of the dialogues of Plato from the Academy, but only those that bore a dogmatic character, while those that presented a more decided Socratic mode of questioning without reaching any decided result, men regarded as authority for Scepticism.

[1] *Adv. Math.* I. 53.

[2] Diog. IV. 6, 33, 34.

[3] Diog. IX. 12, 114.

[4] Diog. IX. 12, 115.

[5] Diog. IV. 6, 33.

[6] Diog. IV. 6, 32.

Sextus does not deny that Arcesilaus was almost a Pyrrhonean, but he claims that his Pyrrhonism was only apparent, and not real, and was used as a cloak to hide his loyalty to the teachings of Plato.[1] As Ariston said of him,[2] "Plato before, Pyrrho behind, Diodorus in the middle." Sextus also characterises the method of Arcesilaus as dialectic,[3] and we know from Cicero that it was his pride to pretend to return to the dialectic of Socrates.

It is interesting to note that Sextus, in his refutation of the position that the Academy is the same as Pyrrhonism, takes up the entire development of Academic thought from the time of Plato till that of Antiochus, and does not limit the argument to Scepticism under Arcesilaus. The claim made by some that the two schools were the same, is stated by him,[4] and the word 'some' probably refers to members of both schools at different periods of their history. Sextus recognises three Academies, although he remarks that some make even a further division, calling that of Philo and Charmides, the fourth, and that of Antiochus and his followers, the fifth.

[1] *Hyp.* I. 234.

[2] Diog. IV. 6, 33.

[3] *Hyp.* I. 234.

[4] *Hyp.* I. 220.

That many in the Academy, and even outside of it, regarded Plato as a Sceptic, and an authority for subsequent Scepticism, we find both from Sextus and Diogenes.[1] As Lewes justly remarks, one could well find authority for Scepticism in the works of Plato, as indeed the Academicians did, but not when the sum total of his teachings was considered. The spirit of Plato's teachings was dogmatic, as Sextus most decidedly recognises, and as Aenesidemus and Menodotus[2] recognised before him.[3] Sextus himself shows us that Plato's idealism and ethical teachings can have nothing in common with Scepticism, for if he accepts the desirability of the virtuous life, and the existence of Providence, he dogmatises; and if he even regards them as probable, he gives preference to one set of ideas over another, and departs from the sceptical character. Sextus characterises the sceptical side of Plato's writings as mental gymnastics,[4] which do not authorise his being called a Sceptic, and affirms that Plato is not a Sceptic, since he prefers some unknown things to others in trustworthiness. The ethical difference underlying the teachings of the Academy and Pyrrhonism, Sextus was very quick to see, and although it is very probable that the part of the *Hypotyposes* which defines the difference between the Academy and Pyrrhonism may be largely quoted from the introduction to Aenesidemus' works, yet Sextus certainly gives these statements the strong stamp of his approval. He condemns the Academy because of the theory that good and evil exist, or if this cannot be decidedly proved, yet that it is more probable that what is called good exists than the contrary.[5]

[1] *Hyp.* I. 221; Diog. IX. 11, 72.

[2] Bekker's edition of *Hyp.* I. 222.

[3] *Hyp.* I. 222.

[4] *Hyp.* I. 223.

[5] *Hyp.* I. 226.

The whole Academic teaching of probabilities contradicted the standpoint of the Sceptics--that our ideas are equal as regards trustworthiness and untrustworthiness,[1] for the Academicians declared that some ideas are probable and some improbable, and they make a difference even in those ideas that they call probable.

Sextus claims that there are three fundamental grounds of difference between Pyrrhonism and the Academy. The first is the doctrine of probability which the Academicians accept in regard to the superior trustworthiness of some ideas over others.[2] The second is the different way in which the two schools follow their teachers. The Pyrrhoneans follow without striving or strong effort, or even strong inclination, as a child follows his teacher, while the Academicians follow with sympathy and assent, as Carneades and Clitomachus affirm.[3] The third difference is in the aim, for the Academicians follow what is probable in life. The Sceptics follow nothing, but live according to laws, customs, and natural feelings undogmatically.[4]

The difference between the later teaching of the Academy and Pyrrhonism is evident, and Sextus treats of it briefly, as not requiring discussion,[5] as Philo taught that the nature of facts is incomprehensible, and Antiochus transferred the Stoa to the Academy. It is therefore evident, from the comparison which we have made, that we do not find in the Academy, with which Scepticism after the death of Timon was so long united, the exact continuance of Pyrrhonism. The philosophical enmity of the two contemporaries, Timon and Arcesilaus, the Academician who had most in common with Pyrrhonism, is an expression of the fundamental incompatibility between the two schools.

[1] *Hyp*. I. 227.

[2] *Hyp*. I. 229.

[3] *Hyp*. I. 230.

[4] *Hyp*. I. 231.

[5] *Hyp*. I. 235.

During all the chequered history of the Academy the dormant idealism was there, underlying the outward development. Although during the time of Arcesilaus and Carneades the difference was so slight as to seem a mere matter of form of expression, yet the different foundations on which the two schools stood was always recognisable. On the one hand there was the germ of idealism which was destined to awake to a new life, and on the other, the attempt at absolute negation which was to result in the final extinction of Pyrrhonism. We find in both, it is true, especially in the time of Arcesilaus, the aim of [Greek: epoche].[1] Both placed great weight on [Greek: isostheneia], or the equal value of opposing arguments.[2] The foundation of the [Greek: epoche] was, however, different in the two cases. Arcesilaus founded his on dialectic, while Pyrrho's was empirical.

[1] *Hyp.* I. 232.

[2] Diog. IX. 73; *Hyp.* II. 130; III. 65.

The Pyrrhonean believed that ideas give us no knowledge of the outer world; the Academic Sceptic believed that we cannot distinguish between true and false ideas, so such knowledge is impossible. The Pyrrhonean denied that truth could exist in ideas because of their contradictory nature, and consequently the existence of all truth, [Greek: meden einai te aletheia epi panton].[1] The Academic Sceptic granted that the truth was possibly contained in ideas, but affirmed that it could never be known to us. The Pyrrhoneans prided themselves on still being seekers, for although ordinary ideas are too contradictory to give knowledge of the outer world, they did not deny that such knowledge might be possible, but simply suspended the judgment regarding it. To the Pyrrhonean the result corresponded to the method. All ideas thus far known revealed nothing of the truth, therefore he still sought. The Academician tried logically to prove that the truth is impossible to find. It is the relation

of the dialectician to the empiricist, and the two varieties of
Scepticism are explained by their difference in origin. In
Pyrrhonism there was no constructive element. In the Academic
Scepsis such an element was found throughout all its history in
the theory of Probability. Arcesilaus himself laid great stress
upon this doctrine, which Sextus carefully shows us[2] is
utterly inconsistent with Pyrrhonism. Arcesilaus plainly teaches
that, having suspended one's judgment in regard to matters of
knowledge, one should control his choices, his refusals, and his
actions by the probable.[3]

[1] Diog. IX. 11, 61.

[2] *Hyp.* I. 229.

[3] Compare Maccoll *Op. cit.* 39.

After Antiochus introduced Eclecticism into the Academy,
Pyrrhonism was the only representative of Greek Scepticism, and
it flourished for over two centuries after our era, and then
also disappeared, no more to exist as a regular philosophical
school.

Having considered at length the essence of Pyrrhonism as
presented by Sextus Empiricus, it now remains to briefly note
the characteristics that formed its strength and weakness, and
the causes of its final downfall. Herbart says that every
philosopher is a Sceptic in the beginning, but every Sceptic
remains always in the beginning. This remark may well be applied
to Pyrrhonism. We find in its teachings many fundamental
philosophical truths which might have formed the beginning of
great philosophical progress, but which were never developed to
any positive results. The teachings of Pyrrhonism were some of

them well fitted to prepare the way to idealism. The great idea of the relativity of **Vorstellungen** is made very prominent by the ten Tropes of [Greek: epoche]. Aenesidemus, in his eight Tropes against aetiology, shows the absurdity of the doctrine of causality when upheld on materialistic grounds. That was to him final, [Greek: epei ouk estai aition.] He could not divine that although the result which he presented was logical, it only led to a higher truth. It was reserved for the greatest of modern philosophers to reveal to the world that causality is a condition, and a necessary condition, of thought. When Aenesidemus proved by his seventh Trope that causality is subjective, he regarded it as fatal to the doctrine; yet this conclusion was a marked step in advance in critical philosophy, although Aenesidemus could not himself see it in all its bearings. The great difference between Aenesidemus and Kant is the difference between the materialist and the believer in subjective reality. Both agreed in the unknown nature of the **Ding an sich**, but this was to the Pyrrhonist the end of all his philosophy; to Kant, however, the beginning.

Pyrrhonism has rendered, notwithstanding its points of fatal weakness, marked service to the world in science, philosophy, ethics, and religion. It quickened scientific thought by emphasising empirical methods of investigation, and by criticising all results founded without sufficient data upon false hypotheses. If, instead of denying the possibility of all science because of the want of a criterion of the truth of phenomena, the Pyrrhonists had comprehended the possibility of a science of phenomena, they might have led the world in scientific progress.[1] Their service to philosophy lay in the stimulus to thought that their frequent attacks on dogmatic beliefs occasioned. Pyrrhonism brought together all the most prominent theories of the old schools of philosophy to test their weakness and expose their contradictions, and this very process of criticism often demonstrated the power of the truth which they contained.

Sextus Empiricus was often charged by the Church Fathers with corrupting religious belief, and yet the greatest service which Pyrrhonism has rendered the world was in religious and ethical lines. This service did not, naturally, consist in destroying belief in absolute truth, as the Sceptic professed to do, but in preparing the way to find it. The bold attacks of Scepticism on all truth led men to investigate ethical and religious teachings, to examine the grounds of their belief, and to put in practical use the right of reason and free discussion.

Scepticism was the antecedent of freedom of conscience and rational criticism,[2] and the absolute right of scientific thought. The Sceptics, however, reaped none of the benefits of their own system. They remained, as it were, always on the threshold of possible progress. With the keys to great discoveries in their hands, the doors of philosophical and scientific advancement were for ever closed to them by the limitations of their own system. The inherent weakness of Pyrrhonism lay in its psychological inconsistency and in its negative character. I think that we may safely say that Pyrrhonism was the most consistent system of Scepticism ever offered to the world, and yet it proves most decidedly that complete Scepticism is psychologically impossible. A man may give up his belief in one set of ideas, and, if they are ideas that are popularly accepted, he will be called a Sceptic, as was the case with Hume. He must, however, replace these ideas by others equally positive, and then he is no longer a Sceptic, but a Dogmatic, for he believes in something.

[1] Compare Lewes *Op. cit.* p. 463.

[2] Compare Chaignet *Op. cit.* p. 460.

We have shown that the greatest thinkers of Pyrrhonism, Pyrrho, Aenesidemus, and Agrippa, were not examples of absolute Scepticism, and although Sextus Empiricus realised what consistency demanded in this respect, and affirmed on almost every page that he was asserting nothing, yet there is not a paragraph of his books in which he does not, after all, dogmatise on some subject. Complete Scepticism is contrary to the fundamental laws of language, as all use of verbs involves some affirmation. The Pyrrhonists realised this, and therefore some of them wrote nothing, like Pyrrho, their leader, and others advocated [Greek: aphasia][1] as one of the doctrines of their system.

[1] *Hyp.* I. 192.

The very aim of Pyrrhonism was an inconsistent one. [Greek: Ataraxia] was only another name for happiness, and in one instance, even, is given as [Greek: hedone], and thus, in spite of themselves, the Sceptics introduced a theory of happiness. Pyrrho, like others of his time, sought the highest good, and thought that he had found it in [Greek: ataraxia], the peace of mind that appears in other systems of philosophy in other forms. The difference of aim between the Pyrrhonists, Stoics, and Epicureans was more apparent than real. To them all philosophy was a path to lead to happiness. The method of Pyrrhonism was, however, negative. Its strength consisted in its attacks on Dogmatism, and not in any positive aim of its own, for its positive side could not be recognised according to its own doctrines. Therefore there was no real development in

Pyrrhonism, for a negative thought cannot be developed.

We find, accordingly, from the time of Pyrrho to Sextus, no growth in breadth of philosophical outlook, only improvement in methods. Philosophical activity can never have doubt as its aim, as that would form, as we have shown, a psychological contradiction. The true essence of Pyrrhonism was passivity, but passivity can never lead to progress. Much of the polemical work of Pyrrhonism prepared the way for scientific progress by providing a vast store of scientific data, but progress was to the Pyrrhonists impossible. They sounded their own scientific death-knell by declaring the impossibility of science, and putting an end to all theories.

The life of all scientific and philosophic progress is in the attempt to find the hidden truth. To the Sceptic there was no truth, and there could be no progress. As progress is a law in the evolution of the human race, so Scepticism as a philosophy could never be a permanent growth, any more than asceticism in religion can be a lasting influence. Both of them are only outgrowths. As the foundation principles of Scepticism were opposed to anything like real growth, it was a system that could never originate anything. Pyrrho taught from the beginning that the Sceptic must live according to law and custom; not, however, because one law or custom is better than another in itself, but simply for the sake of peace. This basis of action was itself a death-blow to all reform in social or political life. It was a selfish, negative way of seeking what was, after all, a positive thing, the [Greek: ataraxia] that the Sceptic desired. Life with the Pyrrhonist was phenomenal, and not phenomenal simply in regard to the outer world, but also subjectively, and no absolute knowledge of the subjective life or of personal existence was possible.

The cause of the downfall of Pyrrhonism lay in the fact that it had nothing to offer to humanity in the place of what it had destroyed. It made no appeal to human sympathies, and ignored all the highest motives to human action. The especial materialistic standpoint from which Pyrrhonism judged all that pertains to knowledge and life shut out the ideal, and all possibility of absolute truth. It was an expression of the philosophic decadence of the age when it flourished, and although it possessed some philosophic worth, yet it bore in itself the causes of its decay.

PYRRHONIC SKETCHES BY SEXTUS EMPIRICUS.

BOOK I.

CHAPTER I.

The Principal Differences between Philosophers.

It is probable that those who seek after anything whatever, will either find it as they continue the search, will deny that it can be found and confess it to be out of reach, or will go on seeking it. Some have said, accordingly, in regard to the things sought in philosophy, that they have found the truth, while others have declared it impossible to find, and still others continue to seek it. Those who think that they have found it are those who are especially called Dogmatics, as for example, the Schools of Aristotle and Epicurus, the Stoics and some others. Those who have declared it impossible to find are Clitomachus, Carneades, with their respective followers, and other Academicians. Those who still seek it are the Sceptics. It appears therefore, reasonable to conclude that the three principal kinds of philosophy are the Dogmatic, the Academic, and the Sceptic. Others may suitably treat of the other Schools, but as for the Sceptical School, we shall now give an outline of it, remarking in advance that in respect to nothing that will be said do we speak positively, that it must be absolutely so, but we shall state each thing historically as it now appears to us.

CHAPTER II.

Ways of Treating Scepticism.

One way of treating the Sceptical philosophy is called general, and the other special. The general method is that by which we set forth the character of Scepticism, declaring what its idea is, what its principles are, its mode of reasoning, its criterion, and its aim. It presents also, the aspects of doubt, [Greek: hoi tropoi tes epoches], and the way in which we should understand the Sceptical formulae, and the distinction between Scepticism and the related Schools of philosophy. The special method, on the contrary, is that by which we 6 speak against each part of so-called philosophy. Let us then treat Scepticism at first in the general way, beginning our delineation with the nomenclature of the Sceptical School.

5

6

CHAPTER III.

The Nomenclature of Scepticism.

The Sceptical School is also called the "Seeking School," from its spirit of research and examination; the "Suspending School," from the condition of mind in which one is left after the search, in regard to the things that he has examined; and the "Doubting School," either because, as some say, the Sceptics doubt and are seeking in regard to everything, or because they never know whether to deny or affirm. It is also called the Pyrrhonean School, because Pyrrho appears to us the best representative of Scepticism, and is more prominent than all who before him occupied themselves with it.

7

CHAPTER IV.

What is Scepticism?

The [Greek: dynamis] of the Sceptical School is to place the phenomenal in opposition to the intellectual "in any way whatever," and thus through the equilibrium of the reasons and things ([Greek: isostheneia ton logon]) opposed to each other, to reach, first the state of suspension of judgment, [Greek: epoche] and afterwards that of imperturbability, [Greek: ataraxia]. We do not use the word [Greek: dynamis] in any

8

9

unusual sense, but simply, meaning the force of the system. By the phenomenal, we understand the sensible, hence we place the intellectual in opposition to it. The phrase "in any way whatever," may refer to the word [Greek: dynamis] in order that we may understand that word in a simple sense as we said, or it may refer to the placing the phenomenal and intellectual in opposition. For we place these in opposition to each other in a variety of ways, the phenomenal to the phenomenal, and the intellectual to the intellectual, or reciprocally, and we say "in any way whatever," in order that all methods of opposition may be included. Or "in any way whatever" may refer to the phenomenal and the intellectual, so that we need not ask how does the phenomenal appear, or how are the thoughts conceived, but that we may understand these things in a simple sense. By "reasons opposed to each other," we do not by any means 10 understand that they deny or affirm anything, but simply that they offset each other. By equilibrium, we mean equality in regard to trustworthiness and untrustworthiness, so that of the reasons that are placed in opposition to each other, one should not excel another in trustworthiness. [Greek: epoche] is a holding back of the opinion, in consequence of which we neither deny nor affirm anything. [Greek: ataraxia] is repose and tranquillity of soul. We shall explain how [Greek: ataraxia] accompanies [Greek: epoche] when we speak of the aim.

CHAPTER V.

The Sceptic.

What is meant by a Pyrrhonean philosopher can be understood from the idea of the Sceptical School. He is a Pyrrhonean, namely, who identifies himself with this system.

11

CHAPTER VI.

The Origin of Scepticism.

Scepticism arose in the beginning from the hope of attaining [Greek: ataraxia]; for men of the greatest talent were perplexed by the contradiction of things, and being at a loss what to believe, began to question what things are true, and what false, hoping to attain [Greek: ataraxia] as a result of the decision. The fundamental principle of the Sceptical system is especially this, namely, to oppose every argument by one of equal weight, for it seems to us that in this way we finally reach the position where we have no dogmas.

12

CHAPTER VII.

Does the Sceptic Dogmatise?

We say that the Sceptic does not dogmatise. We do not say 13 this, meaning by the word dogma the popular assent to certain things rather than others (for the Sceptic does assent to feelings that are a necessary result of sensation, as for example, when he is warm or cold, he cannot say that he thinks he is not warm or cold), but we say this, meaning by dogma the acceptance of any opinion in regard to the unknown things investigated by science. For the Pyrrhonean assents to nothing that is unknown. Furthermore, he does not dogmatise even when 14 he utters the Sceptical formulae in regard to things that are unknown, such as "Nothing more," or "I decide nothing," or any of the others about which we shall speak later. For the one who dogmatises regards the thing about which he is said to dogmatise, as existing in itself; the Sceptic does not however regard these formulae as having an absolute existence, for he assumes that the saying "All is false," includes itself with other things as false, and likewise the saying "Nothing is true"; in the same way "Nothing more," states that together with other things it itself is nothing more, and cancels itself therefore, as well as other things. We say the same also in regard to the other Sceptical expressions. In short, if he who 15 dogmatises, assumes as existing in itself that about which he dogmatises, the Sceptic, on the contrary, expresses his sayings in such a way that they are understood to be themselves included, and it cannot be said that he dogmatises in saying these things. The principal thing in uttering these formulae is that he says what appears to him, and communicates his own feelings in an unprejudiced way, without asserting anything in regard to external objects.

CHAPTER VIII.

Is Scepticism a Sect?

We respond in a similar way if we are asked whether Scepticism is a sect or not. If the word sect is defined as meaning a body of persons who hold dogmas which are in conformity with each other, and also with phenomena, and dogma means an assent to anything that is unknown, then we reply that we have no sect. If, however, one means by sect, a school which follows a certain line of reasoning based on phenomena, and that reasoning shows how it is possible to apparently live rightly, not understanding "rightly" as referring to virtue only, but in a broader sense; if, also, it leads one to be able to suspend the judgment, then we reply that we have a sect. For we follow a certain kind of reasoning which is based upon phenomena, and which shows us how to live according to the habits, laws, and teachings of the fatherland, and our own feelings.

16

17

CHAPTER IX.

Does the Sceptic Study Natural Science?

We reply similarly also to the question whether the Sceptic 18
should study natural science. For we do not study natural
science in order to express ourselves with confidence regarding
any of the dogmas that it teaches, but we take it up in order to
be able to meet every argument by one of equal weight, and also
for the sake of [Greek: ataraxia]. In the same way we study the
logical and ethical part of so-called philosophy.

CHAPTER X.

Do the Sceptics deny Phenomena?

Those who say that the Sceptics deny phenomena appear to me to 19
be in ignorance of our teachings. For as we said before, we do
not deny the sensations which we think we have, and which lead
us to assent involuntarily to them, and these are the phenomena.
When, however, we ask whether the object is such as it appears
to be, while we concede that it appears so and so, we question,
not the phenomenon, but in regard to that which is asserted of
the phenomenon, and that is different from doubting the
phenomenon itself. For example, it appears to us that honey is
sweet. This we concede, for we experience sweetness through 20

sensation. We doubt, however, whether it is sweet by reason of its essence, which is not a question of the phenomenon, but of that which is asserted of the phenomenon. Should we, however, argue directly against the phenomena, it is not with the intention of denying their existence, but to show the rashness of the Dogmatics. For if reasoning is such a deceiver that it well nigh snatches away the phenomena from before your eyes, how should we not distrust it in regard to things that are unknown, so as not to rashly follow it?

CHAPTER XI.

The Criterion of Scepticism.

It is evident that we pay careful attention to phenomena from what we say about the criterion of the Sceptical School. The word criterion is used in two ways. First, it is understood as a proof of existence or non-existence, in regard to which we shall speak in the opposing argument. Secondly, when it refers to action, meaning the criterion to which we give heed in life, in doing some things and refraining from doing others, and it is about this that we shall now speak. We say, consequently, that the criterion of the Sceptical School is the phenomenon, and in calling it so, we mean the idea of it. It cannot be doubted, as it is based upon susceptibility and involuntary feeling. Hence no one doubts, perhaps, that an object appears so and so, but one questions if it is as it appears. Therefore, as we cannot be entirely inactive as regards the observances of daily life, we live by giving heed to phenomena, and in an

21

22

unprejudiced way. But this observance of what pertains to the 23
daily life, appears to be of four different kinds. Sometimes it
is directed by the guidance of nature, sometimes by the
necessity of the feelings, sometimes by the tradition of laws
and of customs, and sometimes by the teaching of the arts. It is
directed by the guidance of nature, for by nature we are 24
capable of sensation and thought; by the necessity of the
feelings, for hunger leads us to food, and thirst to drink; by
the traditions of laws and customs, for according to them we
consider piety a good in daily life, and impiety an evil; by the
teaching of the arts, for we are not inactive in the arts we
undertake. We say all these things, however, without expressing
a decided opinion.

CHAPTER XII.

What is the aim of Scepticism?

It follows naturally in order to treat of the aim of the 25
Sceptical School. An aim is that for which as an end all things
are done or thought, itself depending on nothing, or in other
words, it is the ultimatum of things to be desired. We say,
then, that the aim of the Sceptic is [Greek: ataraxia] in those
things which pertain to the opinion, and moderation in the
things that life imposes. For as soon as he began to 26
philosophise he wished to discriminate between ideas, and to
understand which are true and which are false, in order to
attain [Greek: ataraxia]. He met, however, with contradictions
of equal weight, and, being unable to judge, he withheld his

opinion; and while his judgment was in suspension [Greek: ataraxia] followed, as if by chance, in regard to matters of opinion. For he who is of the opinion that anything is either good or bad by nature is always troubled, and when he does not possess those things that seem to him good he thinks that he is tortured by the things which are by nature bad, and pursues those that he thinks to be good. Having acquired them, however, he falls into greater perturbation, because he is excited beyond reason and without measure from fear of a change, and he does everything in his power to retain the things that seem to him good. But he who is undecided, on the contrary, regarding things that are good and bad by nature, neither seeks nor avoids anything eagerly, and is therefore in a state of [Greek: ataraxia]. For that which is related of Apelles the painter happened to the Sceptic. It is said that as he was once painting a horse he wished to represent the foam of his mouth in the picture, but he could not succeed in doing so, and he gave it up and threw the sponge at the picture with which he had wiped the colors from the painting. As soon, however, as it touched the picture it produced a good copy of the foam. The Sceptics likewise hoped to gain [Greek: ataraxia] by forming judgments in regard to the anomaly between phenomena and the things of thought, but they were unable to do this, and so they suspended their judgment; and while their judgment was in suspension [Greek: ataraxia] followed, as if by chance, as the shadow follows a body. Nevertheless, we do not consider the Sceptic wholly undisturbed, but he is disturbed by some things that are inevitable. We confess that sometimes he is cold and thirsty, and that he suffers in such ways. But in these things even the ignorant are beset in two ways, from the feelings themselves, and not less also from the fact that they think these conditions are bad by nature. The Sceptic, however, escapes more easily, as he rejects the opinion that anything is in itself bad by nature.

Therefore we say that the aim of the Sceptic is [Greek: ataraxia] in matters of opinion, and moderation of feeling in those things that are inevitable. Some notable Sceptics have added also suspension of judgment in investigation.

CHAPTER XIII.

The General Method of Scepticism.

Since we have said that [Greek: ataraxia] follows the suspension of judgment in regard to everything, it behooves us to explain how the suspension of judgment takes place. Speaking in general it takes place through placing things in opposition to each other. We either place phenomena in opposition to phenomena, or the intellectual in opposition to the intellectual, or reciprocally. For example, we place phenomena in opposition to phenomena when we say that this tower appears round from a distance but square near by; the intellectual in opposition to the intellectual, when to the one who from the order of the heavens builds a tower of reasoning to prove that a providence exists, we oppose the fact that adversity often falls to the good and prosperity to the evil, and that therefore we draw the conclusion that there is no providence. The intellectual is placed in opposition to phenomena, as when Anaxagoras opposed the fact that snow is white, by saying that snow is frozen water, and, as water is black, snow must also be black. Likewise we sometimes place the present in opposition to the present, similarly to the above-mentioned cases, and sometimes also the present in

31

32

33

opposition to the past or the future. As for example, when someone proposes an argument to us that we cannot refute, we say to him, "Before the founder of the sect to which you belong 34 was born, the argument which you propose in accordance with it had not appeared as a valid argument, but was dormant in nature, so in the same way it is possible that its refutation also exists in nature, but has not yet appeared to us, so that it is not at all necessary for us to agree with an argument that now seems to be strong." In order to make it clearer to us what 35 we mean by these oppositions, I will proceed to give the Tropes ([Greek: tropoi]), through which the suspension of judgment is produced, without asserting anything about their meaning or their number, because they may be unsound, or there may be more than I shall enumerate.

CHAPTER XIV.

The Ten Tropes.

Certain Tropes were commonly handed down by the older Sceptics, 36 by means of which [Greek: epoche] seems to take place. They are ten in number, and are called synonymously [Greek: logoi] and [Greek: tropoi]. They are these: The first is based upon the differences in animals; the second upon the differences in men; the third upon the difference in the constitution of the organs of sense; the fourth upon circumstances; the fifth upon position, distance, and place; the sixth upon mixtures; the seventh upon the quantity and constitution of objects; the eighth upon relation; the ninth upon frequency or rarity of 37 occurences; the tenth upon systems, customs, laws, mythical beliefs, and dogmatic opinions. We make this order ourselves. These Tropes come under three general heads: the standpoint of the judge, the standpoint of the thing judged, and the standpoint of both together. Under the standpoint of the judge come the first four, for the judge is either an animal, or a man, or a sense, and exists under certain circumstances. Under the standpoint of that which is judged, come the seventh and the tenth. Under the one composed of both together, come the fifth and the sixth, the eighth and the ninth. Again, these three divisions are included under the Trope of relation, because that is the most general one; it includes the three special divisions, and these in turn include the ten. We say these things in regard to their probable number, and we proceed in the following chapter to speak of their meaning.

THE FIRST TROPE.

The first Trope, we said, is the one based upon the differences in animals, and according to this Trope, different animals do not get the same ideas of the same objects through the senses. This we conclude from the different origin of the animals, and also from the difference in the constitution of their bodies. In regard to the difference in origin, some animals originate without mixture of the sexes, while others originate through sexual intercourse. Of those which originate without intercourse of the sexes, some come from fire, as the little animals which appear in the chimneys, others from stagnant water, as musquitoes, others from fermented wine, as the stinging ants, others from the earth, others from the mud, like the frogs, others from slime, as the worms, others from donkeys, as the beetles, others from cabbage, as caterpillars,

others from fruit, as the gall insect from the wild figs, others
from putrified animals, as bees from bulls, and wasps from
horses. Again, of those originating from intercourse of the   42
sexes, some come from animals of the same kind, as in most
cases, and others from those of different kinds, as mules.
Again, of animals in general, some are born alive, as men,
others from eggs, as birds, and others are born a lump of flesh,
as bears. It is probable therefore, that the inequalities and   43
differences in origin cause great antipathies in the animals,
and the result is incompatibility, discord, and conflict between
the sensations of the different animals. Again, the differences
in the principal parts of the body, especially in those 44
fitted by nature to judge and to perceive, may cause the
greatest differences in their ideas of objects, according to the
differences in the animals themselves. As for example, those who
have the jaundice call that yellow which appears to us white,
and those who have bloodshot eyes call it blood-red.
Accordingly, as some animals have yellow eyes, and others
blood-shot ones, and still others whitish ones, and others eyes
of other colors, it is probable, I think, that they have a
different perception of colors. Furthermore, when we look
steadily at the sun for a long time, and then look down at a   45
book, the letters seem to us gold colored, and dance around. Now
some animals have by nature a lustre in their eyes, and these
emit a fine and sparkling light so that they see at night, and
we may reasonably suppose that external things do not appear the
same to them as to us. Jugglers by lightly rubbing the wick   46
of the lamp with metal rust, or with the dark yellow fluid of
the sepia, make those who are present appear now copper-colored
and now black, according to the amount of the mixture used; if
this be so it is much more reasonable to suppose that because of
the mixture of different fluids in the eyes of animals, their
ideas of objects would be different. Furthermore, when we   47

press the eye on the side, the figures, forms and sizes of things seen appear elongated and narrow. It is therefore probable that such animals as have the pupil oblique and long, as goats, cats, and similar animals, have ideas different from those of the animals which have a round pupil. Mirrors according to their different construction, sometimes show the external object smaller than reality, as concave ones, and sometimes long and narrow, as the convex ones do; others show the head of the one looking into it down, and the feet up. As some of the vessels around the eye fall entirely outside the eye, on account of their protuberance, while others are more sunken, and still others are placed in an even surface, it is probable that for this reason also the ideas vary, and dogs, fishes, lions, men, and grasshoppers do not see the same things, either of the same size, or of similar form, but according to the impression on the organ of sight of each animal respectively. The same thing is true in regard to the other senses; for how can it be said that shell-fish, birds of prey, animals covered with spines, those with feathers and those with scales would be affected in the same way by the sense of touch? and how can the sense of hearing perceive alike in animals which have the narrowest auditory passages, and in those that are furnished with the widest, or in those with hairy ears and those with smooth ones? For we, even, hear differently when we partially stop up the ears, from what we do when we use them naturally. The sense of smell also varies according to differences in animals, since even our sense of smell is affected when we have taken cold and the phlegm is too abundant, and also when parts around our head are flooded with too much blood, for we then avoid odors that seem agreeable to others, and feel as if we were injured by them. Since also some of the animals are moist by nature and full of secretions, and others are very full of blood, and still others have either yellow or black bile

prevalent and abundant, it is reasonable because of this to
think that odorous things appear different to each one of them.
And it is the same in regard to things of taste, as some   52
animals have the tongue rough and dry and others very moist. We
too, when we have a dry tongue in fever, think that whatever we
take is gritty, bad tasting, or bitter; and this we experience
because of the varying degrees of the humors that are said to be
in us. Since, then, different animals have different organs for
taste, and a greater or less amount of the various humors, it
can well be that they form different ideas of the same objects
as regards their taste. For just as the same food on being   53
absorbed becomes in some places veins, in other places arteries,
and in other places bones, nerves, or other tissues, showing
different power according to the difference of the parts
receiving it; just as the same water absorbed by the trees
becomes in some places bark, in other places branches, and in
other places fruit, perhaps a fig or a pomegranate, or something
else; just as the breath of the musician, one and the same   54
when blown into the flute, becomes sometimes a high tone and
sometimes a low one, and the same pressure of the hand upon the
lyre sometimes causes a deep tone and sometimes a high tone, so
it is natural to suppose that external objects are regarded
differently according to the different constitution of the
animals which perceive them. We may see this more clearly in   55
the things that are sought for and avoided by animals. For
example, myrrh appears very agreeable to men and intolerable to
beetles and bees. Oil also, which is useful to men, destroys
wasps and bees if sprinkled on them; and sea-water, while it is
unpleasant and poisonous to men if they drink it, is most
agreeable and sweet to fishes. Swine also prefer to wash in vile
filth rather than in pure clean water. Furthermore, some   56
animals eat grass and some eat herbs; some live in the woods,
others eat seeds; some are carnivorous, and others lactivorous;

some enjoy putrified food, and others fresh food; some raw food and others that which is prepared by cooking; and in general that which is agreeable to some is disagreeable and fatal to others, and should be avoided by them. Thus hemlock makes the 57 quail fat, and henbane the hogs, and these, as it is known, enjoy eating lizards; deer also eat poisonous animals, and swallows, the cantharidae. Moreover, ants and flying ants, when swallowed by men, cause discomfort and colic; but the bear, on the contrary, whatever sickness he may have, becomes stronger by devouring them. The viper is benumbed if one twig of the oak 58 touches it, as is also the bat by a leaf of the plane-tree. The elephant flees before the ram, and the lion before the cock, and seals from the rattling of beans that are being pounded, and the tiger from the sound of the drum. Many other examples could be given, but that we may not seem to dwell longer than is necessary on this subject, we conclude by saying that since the same things are pleasant to some and unpleasant to others, and the pleasure and displeasure depend on the ideas, it must be that different animals have different ideas of objects. And since the same things appear different according to the 59 difference in the animals, it will be possible for us to say how the external object appears to us, but as to how it is in reality we shall suspend our judgment. For we cannot ourselves judge between our own ideas and those of other animals, being ourselves involved in the difference, and therefore much more in need of being judged than being ourselves able to judge. And furthermore, we cannot give the preference to our own mental 60 representations over those of other animals, either without evidence or with evidence, for besides the fact that perhaps there is no evidence, as we shall show, the evidence so called will be either manifest to us or not. If it is not manifest to us, then we cannot accept it with conviction; if it is manifest to us, since the question is in regard to what is manifest to animals, and we use as evidence that which is manifest to us who are animals, then it is to be questioned if it is true as it is manifest to us. It is absurd, however, to try to base the 61 questionable on the questionable, because the same thing is to be believed and not to be believed, which is certainly impossible. The evidence is to be believed in so far as it will furnish a proof, and disbelieved in so far as it is itself to be proved. We shall therefore have no evidence according to which we can give preference to our own ideas over those of so-called irrational animals. Since therefore ideas differ according to the difference in animals, and it is impossible to judge them, it is necessary to suspend the judgment in regard to external objects.

Have the So-called Irrational Animals Reason?

We continue the comparison of the so-called irrational animals 62 with man, although it is needless to do so, for in truth we do not refuse to hold up to ridicule the conceited and bragging Dogmatics, after having given the practical arguments. Now most 63 of our number were accustomed to compare all the irrational animals together with man, but because the Dogmatics playing upon words say that the comparison is unequal, we carry our ridicule farther, although it is most superfluous to do so, and fix the discussion on one animal, as the dog, if it suits you, which seems to be the most contemptible animal; for we shall even then find that animals, about which we are speaking, are not inferior to us in respect to the trustworthiness of their perceptions. Now the Dogmatics grant that this animal is 64 superior to us in sense perception, for he perceives better through smell than we, as by this sense he tracks wild animals that he cannot see, and he sees them quicker with his eyes than we do, and he perceives them more acutely by hearing. Let us also consider reasoning, which is of two kinds, reasoning in thought and in speech. Let us look first to that of thought. This kind of reasoning, judging from the teachings of those Dogmatics who are now our greatest opponents, those of the Stoa, seems to fluctuate between the following things: the choice of the familiar, and avoidance of the alien; the knowledge of the arts that lead to this choice; and the comprehension of those virtues that belong to the individual nature, as regards the feelings. The dog then, upon whom it was decided to fix the argument as an example, makes a choice of things suitable to him, and avoids those that are harmful, for he hunts for food, but draws back when the whip is lifted up; he possesses also an art by which he procures the things that are suitable for him, the art of hunting. He is not also without virtue; since the true nature of justice is to give to every one according to his merit, as the dog wags his tail to those who belong to the family, and to those who behave well to him, guards them, and keeps off strangers and evil doers, he is surely not without justice. Now if he has this virtue, since the virtues follow each other in turn, he has the other virtues also, which the wise men say, most men do not possess. We see the dog also brave in warding off attacks, and sagacious, as Homer testified when he represented Odysseus as unrecognised by all in his house, and recognised only by Argos, because the dog was not deceived by the physical change in the man, and had not lost the [Greek: phantasia kataleptike] which he proved that he had kept better than the men had. But according to Chrysippus even, who most attacked the irrational animals, the dog takes a part in the dialectic about which so much is said. At any rate, the man above referred to said that the dog follows the fifth of the several non-apodictic syllogisms, for when he comes to a meeting of three roads, after seeking the scent in the two roads, through which his prey has not passed, he presses forward quickly in the third without scenting it. For the dog reasons in this way, potentially said the man of olden time; the animal passed through this, or this, or this; it was neither through this nor this, therefore it was through this. The dog also understands his own sufferings and mitigates them. As soon as 70 a sharp stick is thrust into him, he sets out to remove it, by rubbing his foot on the ground, as also with his teeth; and if ever he has a wound anywhere, for the reason that uncleansed wounds are difficult to cure, and those that are cleansed are easily cured, he gently wipes off the collected matter; and 71 he observes the Hippocratic advice exceedingly well, for since quiet is a relief for the foot, if he has ever a wound in the foot, he lifts it up, and keeps it undisturbed as much as possible. When he is troubled by disturbing humours, he eats grass, with which he vomits up that which was unfitting, and recovers. Since therefore it has been shown that the animal 72 that we fixed the argument upon for the sake of an example, chooses that which is suitable for him, and avoids what is harmful, and that he has an art by which he provides what is suitable, and that he comprehends his own sufferings and mitigates them, and that he is not without virtue, things in which perfection of reasoning in thought consists, so according to this it would seem that the dog has reached perfection. It is for this reason, it appears to me, that some philosophers have honoured themselves with the name of this animal. In regard to reasoning in speech, it is not necessary at present to bring 73 the matter in question. For some of the Dogmatics, even, have put this aside, as opposing the acquisition of virtue, for which reason they practiced silence when studying. Besides, let it be supposed that a man is dumb, no one would say that he is consequently irrational. However, aside from this, we see after all, that animals, about which we are speaking, do produce human sounds, as the jay and some others. Aside from this also, even if we do not understand the sounds of the so-called irrational irrational animals, it is not at all unlikely that they converse, and that we do not understand their conversation. For when we hear the language of foreigners, we do not understand but it all seems like one sound to us. Furthermore, we hear dogs giving out one kind of sound when they are resisting someone, and another sound when they howl, and another when they are beaten, and a different kind when they wag their tails, and generally speaking, if one examines into this, he will find a great difference in the sounds of this and other animals under different circumstances; so that in all likelihood, it may be said that the so-called irrational animals partake also in spoken language. If then, they are not inferior to men in the accuracy of their perceptions, nor in reasoning in thought, nor in reasoning by speech, as it is superfluous to say, then they are not more untrustworthy than we are, it seems to me, in regard to their ideas. Perhaps it would be possible to prove this, should we direct the argument to each of the irrational animals in turn. As for example, who would not say that the birds are distinguished for shrewdness, and make use of articulate speech? for they not only know the present but the future, and this they augur to those that are able to understand it, audibly as well as in other ways. I have made this comparison superfluously, as I pointed out above, as I think I had sufficiently shown before, that we cannot consider our own ideas superior to those of the irrational animals. In short, if the irrational animals are not more untrustworthy than we in regard to the judgment of their ideas, and the ideas are different according to the difference in the animals, I shall be able to say how each object appears to me, but in regard to what it is by nature I shall be obliged to suspend my judgment.

THE SECOND TROPE.

Such is the first Trope of [Greek: epoche]. The second, we said above, is based upon the differences in men. For even if one assent to the hypothesis that men are more trustworthy than the irrational animals, we shall find that doubt arises as soon as we consider our own differences. For since man is said to be composed of two things, soul and body, we differ from each other in respect to both of these things; for example, as regards the body, we differ both in form and personal peculiarities. For the body of a Scythian differs from the body of an Indian in form, the difference resulting, it is said, from the different control of the humors. According to different control of the humors, differences in ideas arise also, as we represented under the first Trope. For this reason there is certainly a great difference among men in the choice and avoidance of external things. The Indians delight in different things from our own people, and the enjoyment of different things is a sign that different ideas are received of the external objects. We differ in personal peculiarities, as some digest beef better than the little fish from rocky places, and some are affected with purging by the weak wine of Lesbos. There was, they say, an old woman in Attica who could drink thirty drachmas of hemlock without danger, and Lysis took four drachmas of opium unhurt, and Demophon, Alexander's table waiter, shivered when he was in the sun or in a hot bath, and felt warm in the shade; Athenagoras also, from Argos, did not suffer harm if stung by scorpions and venomous spiders; the so-called Psylli were not injured when bitten by snakes or by the aspis, and the Tentyrites among the Egyptians are not harmed by the crocodiles around them; those also of the Ethiopians who live on the Hydaspes river, opposite Meroe, eat scorpions and serpents, and similar things without danger; Rufinus in Chalcis could drink hellebore without vomiting or purging, and he enjoyed and digested it as something to which he was accustomed; Chrysermos, the Herophilian, ran the risk of stomach-ache if he ever took pepper, and Soterichus, the surgeon, was seized by purging if he perceived the odor of roasting shad; Andron, the Argive, was so free from thirst that he could travel even through the waterless Libya without looking for a drink; Tiberius, the emperor, saw in the dark, and Aristotle tells the story of a certain Thracian, who thought that he saw the figure of a man always going before him as a guide. While therefore such a difference exists in men in regard to the body, and we must be satisfied with referring to a few only of the many examples given by the Dogmatics, it is probable that men also differ from each other in respect to the soul itself, for the body is a kind of type of the soul, as the physiognomical craft also shows. The best example of the numerous and infinite differences of opinion among men is the contradiction in the sayings of the Dogmatics, not only about other things, but about what it is well to seek and to avoid. The poets have also fittingly spoken about this, for Pindar said--

> "One delights in getting honors and crowns through storm-footed horses,
> Another in passing life in rooms rich in gold,
> Another still, safe travelling enjoys, in a swift ship, on a wave of the sea."

And the poet says--

> "One man enjoys this, another enjoys that."

The tragedies also abound in such expressions, for instance, it is said--

"If to all, the same were good and wise,
Quarrels and disputes among men would not have been."

And again--

"It is awful indeed, that the same thing some mortals
should please,
And by others be hated."

Since therefore the choice and the avoidance of things, 87
depends on the pleasure and displeasure which they give, and the pleasure and displeasure have their seat in perception and ideas, when some choose the things that others avoid, it is logical for us to conclude that they are not acted upon similarly by the same things, for otherwise they would have chosen or avoided alike. Now if the same things act upon different men differently, on account of the difference in the men, for this cause also suspension of the judgment may reasonably be introduced, and we may perhaps say how each object appears to us, and what its individual differences are, but we shall not be able to declare what it is as to the nature of its essence. For we must either believe all men or some men; but 88
to believe all is to undertake an impossibility, and to accept things that are in opposition to each other. If we believe some only, let someone tell us with whom to agree, for the Platonist would say with Plato, the Epicurean with Epicurus, and others would advise in a corresponding manner; and so as they disagree, with no one to decide, they bring us round again to the suspension of judgment. Furthermore, he who tells us to agree 89
with the majority proposes something childish, as no one could go to all men and find out what pleases the majority, for it is

possible that in some nations which we do not know the things which to us are rare are common to the majority, and those things which happen commonly to us are rare. As for example, it might happen that the majority should not suffer when bitten by venomous spiders, or that they should seldom feel pain, or have other personal peculiarities similar to those spoken of above. It is necessary therefore to suspend the judgment on account of the differences in men.

THE THIRD TROPE.

While, however, the Dogmatics are conceited enough to think that they should be preferred to other men in the judgement of things, we know that their claim is absurd, for they themselves form a part of the disagreement; and if they give themselves preference in this way in the judgment of phenomena, they beg the question before they begin the judgment, as they trust the judgment to themselves. Nevertheless, in order that we should reach the result of the suspension of judgment by limiting the argument to one man, one who for example they deem to be wise, let us take up the third Trope. This is the one that is based upon differences in perception. That the perceptions differ from each other is evident. For example, paintings seem to have hollows and prominences to the sense of sight, but not to the sense of touch, and honey to the tongue of some people appears pleasant, but unpleasant to the eyes; therefore it is impossible to say whether it is really pleasant or unpleasant. In regard to myrrh it is the same, for it delights the sense of smell, but disgusts the sense of taste. Also in regard to euphorbium, since it is harmful to the eyes and harmless to all the rest of the body, we are not able to say whether it is really harmless to bodies or not, as far as its own nature is concerned. Rain-water, too, is useful to the eyes, but it makes the trachea and the lungs rough, just as oil does, although it soothes the skin; and the sea-torpedo placed on the extremities makes them numb, but is harmless when placed on the rest of the body. Wherefore we cannot say what each of these things is by nature. It is possible only to say how it appears each time. We could cite more examples than these, but in order not to spend too long in laying out the plan of this book we shall simply say the following: Each of the phenomena perceived by us seems to present itself in many forms, as the apple, smooth, fragrant, sweet, yellow. Now it is not known whether it has in reality only those qualities which appear to us, or if it has only one quality, but appears different on account of the different constitution of the sense organs, or if it has more qualities than appear to us, but some of them do not affect us. That it has only one quality might be concluded from what we have said about the food distributed in bodies, and the water distributed in trees, and the breath in the flute and syrinx, and in similar instruments; for it is possible that the apple also has only one quality, but appears different on account of the difference in the sense organs by which it is perceived. On the other hand, that the apple has more qualities than those that appear to us, can be argued in this way: Let us imagine someone born with the sense of touch, of smell, and of taste, but neither hearing nor seeing. He will then assume that neither anything visible nor anything audible exists at all, but only the three kinds of qualities which he can apprehend. It is possible then that as we have only the five senses, we apprehend only those qualities of the apple which we are able to grasp, but it may be supposed that other qualities exist which would affect other sense organs if we possessed them; as it is, we do not feel the sensations which would be felt through them. But nature, one will say, has brought the senses into harmony with the objects to be perceived. What kind of nature? Among the Dogmatics a great difference of opinion reigns about the real existence of nature anyway; for he who decides whether there is a nature or not, if he is an uneducated man, would be according to them untrustworthy; if he is a philosopher, he is a part of the disagreement, and is himself to be judged, but is not a judge. In short, if it is possible that only those qualities exist in the apple which we seem to perceive, or that more than these are there, or that not even those which we perceive exist, it will be unknown to us what kind of a thing the apple is. The same argument holds for other objects of perception. If, however, the senses do not comprehend the external world, the intellect cannot comprehend it either, so that for this reason also it will appear that the suspension of judgment follows in regard to external objects. 99

THE FOURTH TROPE.

In order to attain to [Greek: epoche] by fixing the argument on each separate sense, or even by putting aside the senses altogether, we take up the fourth Trope of [Greek: epoche]. This is the one based upon circumstances, and by circumstances we mean conditions. This Trope comes under consideration, we may say, with regard to conditions that are according to nature, or contrary to nature; such as waking or sleeping, the age of life, moving or keeping still, hating or loving, need or satiety, drunkenness or sobriety, predispositions, being courageous or afraid, sorrowing or rejoicing. For example, things appear different as they are according to nature, or contrary to it; as for instance, the insane and those inspired by a god, think that they hear gods, while we do not; in like manner they often say that they perceive the odor of storax or frankincense, or the 100 101 like, and many other things which we do not perceive. Water, also, that seems lukewarm to us, if poured over places that are inflamed, will feel hot, and a garment that appears orange-coloured to those that have blood-shot eyes, would not look so to me, and the same honey appears sweet to me, but bitter to those who have the jaundice. If one should say 102 that those who are not in a natural state have unusual ideas of objects, because of the intermingling of certain humors, then one must also say, that it may be that objects which are really what they seem to be to those who are in an unnatural condition, appear different to those who are in health, for even those who are in health have humors that are mixed with each other. For to 103 give to one kind of fluid a power to change objects, and not to another kind, is a fiction of the mind; for just as those who are in health are in a condition that is natural to those who are in health, and contrary to the nature of those who are not in health, so also those who are not in health, are in a condition contrary to the nature of those in health, but natural to those not in health, and we must therefore believe that they also are in some respect in a natural condition. Furthermore, 104 in sleep or in waking, the ideas are different, because we do not see things in the same way when we are awake as we do in sleep; neither do we see them in the same way in sleep as we do when awake, so that the existence or non-existence of these things is not absolute, but relative, that is in relation to a sleeping or waking condition. It is therefore probable that we see those things in sleep which in a waking condition do not exist, but they are not altogether non-existent, for they exist in sleep, just as those things which exist when we are awake, exist, although they do not exist in sleep. Furthermore, things 105 present themselves differently according to the age of life, for the same air seems cold to the aged, but temperate to those in their prime, and the same color appears dim to those who are old, and bright to those in their prime, and likewise the same tone seems faint to the former, and audible to the latter. People in different ages are also differently disposed 106 towards things to be chosen or avoided; children, for example, are very fond of balls and hoops, while those in their prime prefer other things, and the old still others, from which it follows that the ideas in regard to the same objects differ in different periods of life. Furthermore, things appear different 107 in a condition of motion and rest, since that which we see at rest when we are still, seems to move when we are sailing by it. There are also differences which depend on liking or 108 disliking, as some detest swine flesh exceedingly, but others eat it with pleasure. As Menander said--

"O how his face appears
Since he became such a man! What a creature!
Doing no injustice would make us also beautiful."

Many also that love ugly women consider them very beautiful Furthermore, there are differences which depend on hunger or 109 satiety, as the same food seems agreeable to those who are hungry, and disagreeable to those who are satisfied. There are also differences depending on drunkenness and sobriety, as that which we consider ugly when we are sober does not appear ugly to us when we are drunk. Again, there are differences depending 110 on predispositions, as the same wine appears sourish to those who have previously eaten dates or dried figs, but agreeable to those who have taken nuts or chickpeas; the vestibule of the bath warms those who enter from without, but cools those who go out, if they rest in it. Furthermore, there are differences 111 depending on being afraid or courageous, as the same thing seems fearful and terrible to the coward, but in no wise so to him who is brave. There are differences, also, depending on being sad or joyful, as the same things are unpleasant to the sad, but pleasant to the joyful. Since therefore the anomalies depending on conditions are so great, and since men are in different conditions at different times, it is perhaps easy to say how each object appears to each man, but not so of what kind it is, because the anomaly is not of a kind to be judged. For he who would pass judgment upon this is either in some one of the conditions mentioned above, or is in absolutely no condition whatever; but to say that he is in no condition at all, as, for example, that he is neither in health nor in illness, that he is neither moving nor quiet, that he is not of any age, and also that he is free from the other conditions, is wholly absurd. But if he judges the ideas while he is in any condition whatever, he is a part of the contradiction, and, besides, he is no genuine critic of external objects, because he is confused by the condition in which he finds himself. Therefore neither can the one who is awake compare the ideas of those who are asleep with those who are awake, nor can he who is in health compare the ideas of the sick with those of the well; for we believe more in the things that are present, and affecting us at present, than in the things not present. In another way, the anomaly in such ideas is impossible to be judged, for whoever prefers one idea to another, and one condition to another, does this either without a criterion and a proof, or with a criterion and a proof; but he can do this neither without them, for he would then be untrustworthy, nor with them; for if he judges ideas, he judges them wholly by a criterion, and he will say that this criterion is either true or false. But if it is false, he will be untrustworthy; if, on the contrary, he says that it is true, he will say that the criterion is true either without proof or with proof. If without proof, he will be untrustworthy; if he says that it is true with proof, it is certainly necessary that the proof be true, or he will be untrustworthy. Now will he say that the proof which he has accepted for the accrediting of the criterion is true, having judged it, or without having judged it? If he says so 116 without judging it, he will be untrustworthy; if he has judged it, it is evident that he will say that he has judged according to some criterion, and we must seek a proof for this criterion, and for that proof a criterion. For the proof always needs a criterion to establish it, and the criterion needs a proof that it may be shown to be true; and a proof can neither be sound without a pre-existing criterion that is true, nor a criterion true without a proof that is shown beforehand to be trustworthy. And so both the criterion and the proof are thrown into the 117 *circulus in probando*, by which it is found that they are both of them untrustworthy, for as each looks for proof from the other, each is as untrustworthy as the other. Since then one cannot prefer one idea to another, either without a proof and a criterion or with them, the ideas that differ according to different conditions cannot be judged, so that the suspension of judgment in regard to the nature of external objects follows through this Trope also.

THE FIFTH TROPE.

The fifth Trope is that based upon position, distance, and 118 place, for, according to each of these, the same things appear different, as for example, the same arcade seen from either end appears curtailed, but from the middle it looks symmetrical on every side; and the same ship appears small and motionless from afar, and large and in motion near by, and the same tower appears round from a distance, but square near by. So much for distance. Now in reference to place, we say that the light 119 of the lamp appears dim in the sun, but bright in the dark; and the same rudder appears broken in the sea, but straight out of it; and the egg in the bird is soft, but in the air hard; and the lyngurion is a fluid in the lynx, but is hard in the air; and the coral is soft in the sea, but hard in the air; and a tone of voice appears different produced by a syrinx, and by a flute, and different simply in the air. Also in reference to position, the same picture leaned back appears smooth, and leaned forward a little seems to have hollows and protuberances, and the necks of doves appear different in color according to the difference in inclination. Since then all phenomena are seen in relation to place, distance, and position, each of which relation makes a great difference with the idea, as we have mentioned, we shall be obliged by this Trope also to come to the suspension of judgment. For he who wishes to give preference to certain ones of these ideas will attempt the impossible. For if he simply makes the decision without proof he will be untrustworthy. If, however, he wishes to make use of a proof, should he say that the proof is false, he contradicts himself, but if he declares the proof to be true, proof of its proof will be demanded of him, and another proof for that, which proof also must be true, and so on to the ***regressus in infinitum***. It is impossible, however, to present proofs ***in infinitum***, so that one will not be able to prove that one idea is to be preferred to another. Since then one cannot either without proof or with proof judge the ideas in question, the suspension of judgment results, and how each thing appears according to this or that position, or this or that distance, or this or that place, we perhaps are able to say, but what it really is it is impossible to declare, for the reasons which we have mentioned.

THE SIXTH TROPE.

The sixth Trope is the one based upon mixtures, according to 124
which we conclude that since no object presents itself alone,
but always together with something else, it is perhaps possible
to say of what nature the mixture is, of the thing itself, and
of that with which it is seen, but of what sort the external
object really is we shall not be able to say. Now it is evident,
I think, that nothing from without is known to us by itself, but
always with something else, and that because of this fact it
appears different. The color of our skin, for example, is 125
different seen in warm air from what it is in cold, and we
could not say what our color really is, only what it is when
viewed under each of these conditions. The same sound appears
different in rare air from what it is in dense, and aromas are
more overpowering in the warm bath and in the sun than they are
in the cold air, and a body surrounded by water is light, but by
air heavy. Leaving aside, however, outer mixtures, our eyes 126
have inside of them coatings and humors. Since then visible
things are not seen without these, they will not be accurately
comprehended, for it is the mixture that we perceive, and for
this reason those who have the jaundice see everything yellow,
and those with bloodshot eyes bloody. Since the same sound
appears different in broad open places from what it does in
narrow and winding ones, and different in pure air and in
impure, it is probable that we do not perceive the tones
unmixed; for the ears have narrow winding passages filled with
vaporous secretions, which it is said gather from places around
the head. Since also there are substances present in the 127
nostrils and in the seat of the sense of taste, we perceive the
things smelled and the things tasted in connection with them,
and not unmixed. So that because of mixture the senses do not

perceive accurately what the external objects are. The intellect 128
even does not do this, chiefly because its guides, the
senses, make mistakes, and perhaps it itself adds a certain
special mixture to those messages communicated by the senses;
for in each place where the Dogmatics think that the ruling
faculty is situated, we see that certain humors are present,
whether one would locate it in the region of the brain, in the
region of the heart, or somewhere else. Since therefore
according to this Trope also, we see that we cannot say anything
regarding the nature of external objects, we are obliged to
suspend our judgment.

THE SEVENTH TROPE.

The seventh Trope is the one which, as we said, is based 129
upon the quantity and constitution of objects, constitution
commonly meaning composition. And it is evident that we are
obliged to suspend our judgment according to this Trope also in
regard to the nature of things. As for example, filings from the
horn of the goat appear white when they are seen separately and
without being put together; put together, however, in the form
of a horn, they look black. And the parts of silver, the filings
that is, by themselves appear black, but as a whole appear
white; and parts of the Taenarus stone look white when ground,
but in the whole stone appear yellow; grains of sand 130
scattered apart from each other appear to be rough, but put
together in a heap, they produce a soft feeling; hellebore taken
fine and downy, causes choking, but it no longer does so when
taken coarse; wine also taken moderately strengthens us, but 131
when taken in excess relaxes the body; food similarly, has a
different effect according to the quantity, at least, it often
disturbs the body when too much is taken, causing dyspepsia and

discharge. We shall be able here also to say of what kind 132
the cutting from the horn is, and what many cuttings put
together are, of what kind a filing of silver is, and what many
of them put together are, of what kind the tiny Taenarus stone,
and what one composed of many small ones is, and in regard to
the grains of sand, and the hellebore, and the wine, and the
food, what they are in relation, but no longer the nature of the
thing by itself, because of the anomaly in the ideas which we
have of things, according to the way in which they are put
together. In general it appears that useful things become 133
harmful when an intemperate use is made of them, and things that
seem harmful when taken in excess, are not injurious in a small
quantity. What we see in the effect of medicines witnesses
especially to this fact, as an exact mixture of simple remedies
makes a compound which is helpful, but sometimes when a very
small inclination of the balance is overlooked, the medicine is
not only not helpful, but very harmful, and often poisonous. So 134
the argument based upon the quantity and constitution of
objects, puts in confusion the existence of external objects.
Therefore this Trope naturally leads us to suspend our judgment,
as we are not able to declare exactly the nature of external
objects.

THE EIGHTH TROPE.

The eighth Trope is the one based upon relation, from which 135
we conclude to suspend our judgment as to what things are
absolutely, in their nature, since every thing is in relation to
something else. And we must bear in mind that we use the word
is incorrectly, in place of *appears*, meaning to say, every
thing *appears* to be in relation. This is said, however, with
two meanings: first, that every thing is in relation to the one

who judges, for the external object, *i.e.* the thing judged, appears to be in relation to the judge; the other way is that every thing is in relation to the things considered together with it, as the relation of the right hand to the left. But we came to the conclusion above, that every thing is in relation to something, as for example, to the one judging; each thing appears in relation to this or that animal, and this or that man, and this or that sense, and in certain circumstances; as regards things considered together, also, each thing appears in relation to this or that mixture, and this or that Trope, and this or that composition, quantity and place. And in another way it is possible to conclude that every thing is in relation to something, as follows: does the being in difference differ from the being in relation, or not? If it does not differ, then it is the same as relation; if it does differ, since every thing which differs is in some relation, for it is said to be in relation to that from which it differs, those things which are in a difference are in a relation to something. Now according to the Dogmatics, some beings belong to the highest genera, others to the lowest species, and others to both genera and species at the same time; all of these are in relation to something, therefore every thing is in relation to something. Furthermore, among things, some things are manifest, and others are hidden, as the Dogmatics themselves say, and the things that make themselves known to us are the phenomena, and the things that are made known to us by the phenomena are the hidden things, for according to the Dogmatics, the phenomena are the outward appearance of the unknown; then that which makes known, and that which is made known, are in relation to something; every thing, therefore, is in relation to something. In addition to this, some things are similar to each other, and others are dissimilar, some are equal, and others are unequal. Now these things are in relation to something, therefore every

136

137

138

139

thing is in relation to something, and whoever says that every thing is not in relation to something, himself establishes the fact that every thing is in relation to something, for even in saying that every thing is not in relation to something, he 140 proves it in reference to us, and not in general, by his objections to us. In short, as we have shown that every thing is in relation to something, it is then evident that we shall not be able to say exactly what each object is by nature, but what it appears to be like in relation to something else. It follows from this, that we must suspend our judgment regarding the nature of things.

THE NINTH TROPE.

In regard to the Trope based on the frequency and rarity of 141 events, which we call the ninth of the series, we give the following explanation: The sun is certainly a much more astonishing thing than a comet, but because we see the sun continually and the comet rarely we are so much astonished at the comet that it even seems an omen, while we are not at all astonished at the sun. If, however, we should imagine the sun appearing at rare intervals, and at rare intervals setting, in the first instance suddenly lighting up all things, and in the second casting everything into shade, we should see great astonishment at the sight. An earthquake, too, does not trouble 142 those who experience it for the first time in the same manner as those who have become accustomed to it. How great the astonishment of a man who beholds the sea for the first time! And the beauty of the human body, seen suddenly for the first time, moves us more than if we are accustomed to seeing it. That which is rare seems valuable, while things that are familiar 143 and easily obtained seem by no means so. If, for example, we

should imagine water as rare, of how much greater value would it
seem than all other valuable things! or if we imagine gold as
simply thrown about on the ground in large quantities like
stones, to whom do we think it would be valuable, or by whom
would it be hoarded, as it is now? Since then the same things
according to the frequency or rarity that they are met with seem
to be now valuable and now not so, we conclude that it may be
that we shall be able to say what kind of a thing each of   144
them appears to be according to the frequency or rarity with
which it occurs, but we are not able to say what each external
object is absolutely. Therefore, according to this Trope also,
we suspend our judgment regarding these things.

THE TENTH TROPE.

The tenth Trope is the one principally connected with   145
morals, relating to schools, customs, laws, mythical beliefs,
and dogmatic opinions. Now a school is a choice of a manner of
life, or of something held by one or many, as for example the
school of Diogenes or the Laconians. A law is a written   146
contract among citizens, the transgressor of which is punished.
A custom or habit, for there is no difference, is a common
acceptance of a certain thing by many, the deviator from which
is in no wise punished. For example, it is a law not to commit
adultery, and it is a custom with us [Greek: to me demosia
gynaiki mignusthai]. A mythical belief is a tradition 147
regarding things which never took place, but were invented, as
among others, the tales about Cronus, for many are led to
believe them. A dogmatic opinion is the acceptance of something
that seems to be established by a course of reasoning, or by
some proof, as for example, that atoms are elements of things,
and that they are either homogeneous, or infinitesimal, or of

some other description. Now we place each of these things sometimes in opposition to itself, and sometimes in opposition to each one of the others. For example, we place a custom in opposition to a custom thus: some of the Ethiopians tattoo new-born children, but we do not, and the Persians think it is seemly to have a garment of many colors and reaching to the feet, but we think it not so. The Indians [Greek: tais gynaixi deomosia mignyntai] but most of the other nations consider it a shame. We place a law in opposition to a law in this way: among the Romans he who renounces his paternal inheritance does not pay his father's debts, but among the Rhodians he pays them in any case; and among the Tauri in Scythia it was a law to offer strangers in sacrifice to Artemis, but with us it is forbidden to kill a man near a temple. We place a school in opposition to a school when we oppose the school of Diogenes to that of Aristippus, or that of the Laconians to that of the Italians. We place a mythical belief in opposition to a mythical belief, as by some traditions Jupiter is said to be the father of men and gods, and by others Oceanus, as we say--

148

149

150

"Oceanus father of the gods, and Tethys the mother."

We place dogmatic opinions in opposition to each other, when we say that some declare that there is only one element, but others that they are infinite in number, and some that the soul is mortal, others that it is immortal; and some say that our affairs are directed by the providence of the gods, but others that there is no providence. We place custom in opposition to other things, as for example to a law, when we say that among the Persians it is the custom to practice [Greek: arrenomixiai], but among the Romans it is forbidden by law to do it; by us adultery is forbidden, but among the Massagetae indifference in this respect is allowed by custom, as Eudoxos of Cnidus relates

151

152

in the first part of his book of travels; among us it is
forbidden [Greek: metrasi mignusthai], but among the Persians it
is the custom by preference to marry so; the Egyptians marry
sisters also, which among us is forbidden by law. Further, 153
we place a custom in opposition to a school, when we say that
most men [Greek: anachorountes mignuontai tais heauton gunaixin,
ho de Krates te Hipparchia demosia], and Diogenes went around
with one shoulder bare, but we go around with our customary
clothes. We place a custom in opposition to a mythical 154
belief, as when the myths say that Cronus ate his own children,
while with us it is the custom to take care of our children; and
among us it is the custom to venerate the gods as good, and not
liable to evil, but they are described by the poets as being
wounded, and also as being jealous of each other. We place a
custom in opposition to a dogmatic opinion when we say that 155
it is a custom with us to seek good things from the gods, but
that Epicurus says that the divine pays no heed to us;
Aristippus also held it to be a matter of indifference to wear a
woman's robe, but we consider it shameful. We place a school in
opposition to a law, as according to the law it is not allowed 156
to beat a free and noble born man, but the wrestlers and
boxers strike each other according to the teaching of their
manner of life, and although murder is forbidden, the gladiators
kill each other for the same reason. We place a mythical 157
belief in opposition to a school when we say that, although the
myths say of Hercules that in company with Omphale--

"He carded wool, and bore servitude,"

and did things that not even an ordinary good man would have
done, yet Hercules' theory of life was noble. We place a 158
mythical belief in opposition to a dogmatic opinion when we
say that athletes seeking after glory as a good, enter for its

sake upon a laborious profession, but many philosophers, on the other hand, teach that glory is worthless. We place law in opposition to mythical belief when we say the poets 159 represent the gods as working adultery and sin, but among us the law forbids those things. We place law in opposition to dogmatic opinion when we say that the followers of Chrysippus hold 160 that it is a matter of indifference to marry one's mother or sister, but the law forbids these things. We place a mythical belief in opposition to a dogmatic opinion when we say that 161 the poets represent Jupiter as descending and holding intercourse with mortal women, but the Dogmatics think this was impossible; also that the poet says that Jupiter, on account 162 of his sorrow for Sarpedon, rained drops of blood upon the earth, but it is a dogma of the philosophers that the divine is exempt from suffering; and they deny the myth of the horse-centaurs, giving us the horse-centaur as an example of non-existence. Now we could give many other examples of each 163 of the antitheses mentioned above, but for a brief argument, these are sufficient. Since, however, such anomaly of things is shown by this Trope also, we shall not be able to say what objects are by nature, but only what each thing appears to be like, according to this or that school, or this or that law, or this or that custom, or according to each of the other conditions. Therefore, by this Trope also, we must suspend our judgment in regard to the nature of external objects. Thus we arrive at [Greek: epoche] through the ten Tropes.

CHAPTER XV.

The Five Tropes.

The later Sceptics, however, teach the following five Tropes 164 of [Greek: epoche]: first, the one based upon contradiction; second, the *regressus in infinitum*; third, relation; fourth, the hypothetical; fifth, the *circulus in probando*. The one 165 based upon contradiction is the one from which we find, that in reference to the thing put before us for investigation, a position has been developed which is impossible to be judged, either practically, or theoretically, and therefore, as we are not able to either accept or reject anything, we end in suspending the judgment. The one based upon the regressus 166 in infinitum is that in which we say that the proof brought forward for the thing set before us calls for another proof, and that one another, and so on to infinity, so that, not having anything from which to begin the reasoning, the suspension of judgment follows. The one based upon relation, as we have 167 said before, is that one in which the object appears of this kind or that kind, as related to the judge and to the things regarded together with it, but we suspend our judgment as to what it is in reality. The one based upon hypothesis is 168 illustrated by the Dogmatics, when in the regressus in infinitum they begin from something that they do not found on reason, but which they simply take for granted without proof. The Trope, *circulus in probando*, arises when the thing 169 which ought to prove the thing sought for, needs to be sustained by the thing sought for, and as we are unable to take the one for the proof of the other, we suspend our judgment in regard to both. Now we shall briefly show that it is possible to refer every thing under investigation to one or another of these Tropes, as follows: the thing before us is either sensible or intellectual; difference of opinion exists, however, as to what it is in itself, for some say that only the things of sense are true, others, only those belonging to the understanding, and others say that some things of sense, and some of thought, are true. Now, will it be said that this difference of opinion can be judged or cannot be judged? If it cannot be judged, then we have the result necessarily of suspension of judgment, because it is impossible to express opinion in regard to things about which a difference of opinion exists which cannot be judged. If it can be judged, then we ask how it is to be judged? For example, the sensible, for we shall limit the argument first to this--Is it to be judged by sensible or by intellectual standards? For if it is to be judged by a sensible one, since we are in doubt about the sensible, that will also need something else to sustain it; and if that proof is also something sensible, something else will again be necessary to prove it, and so on *in infinitum*. If, on the contrary, the sensible must be judged by something intellectual, as there is disagreement in regard to the intellectual, this intellectual thing will require also judgment and proof. Now, how is it to be proved? If by something intellectual, it will likewise be thrown into *infinitum*; if by something sensible, as the intellectual has been taken for the proof of the sensible, and the sensible has been taken for that of the intellectual, the circulus in probando is introduced. If, however, in order to escape from this, the one who is speaking to us expects us to take something for granted which has not been proved, in order to prove what follows, the hypothetical Trope is introduced, which provides no way of escape. For if the one who makes the

170

171

172

173

hypothesis is worthy of confidence, we should in every case be no less worthy of confidence in making a contrary hypothesis. If the one who makes the assumption assumes something true, he makes it suspicious by using it as a hypothesis, and not as an established fact; if it is false, the foundation of the reasoning is unsound. If a hypothesis is any help towards a 174 trustworthy result, let the thing in question itself be assumed, and not something else, by which, forsooth, one would establish the thing under discussion. If it is absurd to assume the thing questioned, it is also absurd to assume that upon which it rests. That all things belonging to the senses are also in 175 relation to something else is evident, because they are in relation to those who perceive them. It is clear then, that whatever thing of sense is brought before us, it may be easily referred to one of the five Tropes. And we come to a similar conclusion in regard to intellectual things. For if it should be said that there is a difference of opinion regarding them which cannot be judged, it will be granted that we must suspend the judgment concerning it. In case the difference of opinion 176 can be judged, if it is judged through anything intellectual, we fall into the *regressus in infinitum*, and if through anything sensible into the *circulus in probando*; for, as the sensible is again subject to difference of opinion, and cannot be judged by the sensible on account of the *regressus in infinitum*, it will have need of the intellectual, just as the intellectual has need of the sensible. But he who accepts anything which is hypothetical again is absurd. Intellectual things stand also 177 in relation, because the form in which they are expressed depends on the mind of the thinker, and, if they were in reality exactly as they are described, there would not have been any difference of opinion about them. Therefore the intellectual also is brought under the five Tropes, and consequently it is necessary to suspend the judgment altogether with regard to every thing that is brought before us. Such are the five Tropes taught by the later Sceptics. They set them forth, not to throw out the ten Tropes, but in order to put to shame the audacity of the Dogmatics in a variety of ways, by these Tropes as well as by those.

CHAPTER XVI.

The Two Tropes.

Two other Tropes of [Greek: epoche] are also taught. For as it appears that everything that is comprehended is either comprehended through itself or through something else, it is thought that this fact introduces doubt in regard to all things. And that nothing can be understood through itself is evident, it is said, from the disagreement which exists altogether among the physicists in regard to sensible and intellectual things. I mean, of course, a disagreement which cannot be judged, as we are not able to use a sensible or an intellectual criterion in judging it, for everything that we would take has a part in the disagreement, and is untrustworthy. Nor is it conceded that anything can be comprehended through something else; for if a thing is comprehended through something, that must always in turn be comprehended through something else, and the regressus in infinitum *or the* circulus in probando follow. If, on the contrary, a thing is comprehended through something that one wishes to use as if it had been comprehended through itself, this is opposed to the fact that nothing can be comprehended through itself, according to what we have said. We do not know

178

179

how that which contradicts itself can be comprehended, either through itself or through something else, as no criterion of the truth or of comprehension appears, and signs without proof would be rejected, as we shall see in the next book. So much will suffice for the present about suspension of judgment.

CHAPTER XVII.

What are the Tropes for the overturning of Aetiology?

In the same manner as we teach the Tropes of [Greek: epoche], some set forth Tropes through which we oppose the Dogmatics, by expressing doubt in regard to the aetiology of which they are especially proud. So Aenesidemus teaches eight Tropes, by which he thinks that he can prove all the dogmatic aetiology useless. The first of these Tropes, he said, relates to the character of aetiology in general, which does not give incontestable testimony in regard to phenomena, because it treats of unseen things. The second Trope states that although abundant resources exist by which to investigate the cause of a thing in question, some Dogmatics investigate it in one way only. The third Trope states that the Dogmatics assign causes which do not show any order for things which have taken place in an orderly manner. The fourth Trope states that the Dogmatics, accepting phenomena as they take place, think that they also understand how unseen things take place, although perhaps the unseen things have taken place in the same way as the phenomena, and perhaps in some other way peculiar to themselves. The fifth Trope states that they all, so to speak, assign causes according to their

180

181

182

183

own hypotheses about the elements, but not according to any commonly accepted methods. The sixth states that they often explain things investigated according to their own hypotheses, but ignore opposing hypotheses which have equal probability. The seventh states that they often give reasons for things that 184 not only conflict with phenomena, but also with their own hypotheses. The eighth states that although that which seems manifest, and that which is to be investigated, are often equally inscrutable, they build up a theory from the one about the other, although both are equally inscrutable. It is not impossible, Aenesidemus said also, that some Dogmatics 185 should fail in their theories of causality from other combinations of reasons deducible from the Tropes given above. Perhaps also the five Tropes of [Greek: epoche] are sufficient to refute aetiology, for he who proposes a cause will propose one which is either in harmony with all the sects of philosophy, with Scepticism, and with phenomena, or one that is not. Perhaps, however, it is not possible that a cause should be in harmony with them, for phenomena and unknown things altogether disagree with each other. If it is not in harmony with them, the reason of this will also be demanded of the one who proposed 186 it; and if he accepts a phenomenon as the cause of a phenomenon, or something unknown as the cause of the unknown, he will be thrown into the *regressus in infinitum*; if he uses one cause to account for another one, into the *circulus in probando*; but if he stops anywhere, he will either say that the cause that he proposes holds good so far as regards the things that have been said, and introduce relation, abolishing an absolute standpoint; or if he accepts anything by hypothesis, he will be attacked by us. Therefore it is perhaps possible to put the temerity of the Dogmatics to shame in aetiology by these Tropes.

CHAPTER XVIII.

The Sceptical Formulae.

When we use any one of these Tropes, or the Tropes of [Greek: epoche], we employ with them certain formulae which show the Sceptical method and our own feeling, as for instance, the sayings, "No more," "One must determine nothing," and certain others. It is fitting therefore to treat of these in this place. Let us begin with "No more." 187

CHAPTER XIX.

The Formula "No more."

We sometimes express this as I have given it, and sometimes thus, "Nothing more." For we do not accept the "No more," as some understand it, for the examination of the special, and "Nothing more" for that of the general, but we use "No more" and "Nothing more" without any difference, and we shall at present treat of them as one and the same expression. Now this formula is defective, for as when we say a double one we really mean a double garment, and when we say a broad one we really mean a broad road; so when we say "No more" we mean really no more than this, or in every way the same. But some of the Sceptics use 188

189

instead of the interrogation "No?" the interrogation "What, this rather than this?" using the word "what" in the sense of "what is the reason," so that the formula means, "What is the reason for this rather than for this?" It is a customary thing, however, to use an interrogation instead of a statement, as "Who of the mortals does not know the wife of Jupiter?" and also to use a statement instead of an interrogation, as "I seek where Dion dwells," and "I ask why one should admire a poet." The word "what" is also used instead of "what for" by Menander--"(For) what did I remain behind?" The formula "Not more this than this" expresses our own condition of mind, and signifies that 190 because of the equality of the things that are opposed to each other we finally attain to a state of equilibrium of soul. We mean by equality that equality which appears to us as probable, by things placed in opposition to each other we mean simply things which conflict with each other, and by a state of equilibrium we mean a state in which we do not assent to one thing more than to another. Even if the formula "Nothing 191 more" seems to express assent or denial, we do not use it so, but we use it loosely, and not with accuracy, either instead of an interrogation or instead of saying, "I do not know to which of these I would assent, and to which I would not." What lies before us is to express what appears to us, but we are indifferent to the words by which we express it. This must be understood, however, that we use the formula "Nothing more" without affirming in regard to it that it is wholly sure and true, but we present it as it appears to us.

CHAPTER XX.

Aphasia.

We explain Aphasia as follows: The word [Greek: phasis] is used in two ways, having a general and a special signification. According to the general signification, it expresses affirmation or negation, as "It is day" or "It is not day"; according to the special signification, it expresses an affirmation only, and negations are not called [Greek: phaseis]. Now Aphasia is the opposite of [Greek: phasis] in its general signification, which, as we said, comprises both affirmation and negation. It follows that Aphasia is a condition of mind, according to which we say that we neither affirm nor deny anything. It is evident from this that we do not understand by Aphasia something that inevitably results from the nature of things, but we mean that we now find ourselves in the condition of mind expressed by it in regard to the things that are under investigation. It is necessary to remember that we do not say that we affirm or deny any of those things that are dogmatically stated in regard to the unknown, for we yield assent only to those things which affect our feelings and oblige us to assent to them.   192   193

CHAPTER XXI.

"Perhaps," and "It is possible," and "It may be."

The formulae "Perhaps," and "Perhaps not," and "It is possible," and "It is not possible," and "It may be," and "It may not be," we use instead of "Perhaps it is," and "Perhaps it is not," and "It is possible that it is," and "It is possible that it is not," and "It may be that it is," and "It may be that it is not." That is, we use the formula "It is not possible" for the sake of brevity, instead of saying "It is not possible to be," and "It may not be" instead of "It may not be that it is," and "Perhaps not" instead of "Perhaps it is not." Again, we do not here dispute about words, neither do we question if the formulae mean these things absolutely, but we use them loosely, as I said before. Yet I think it is evident that these formulae express Aphasia. For certainly the formula "Perhaps it is" really includes that which seems to contradict it, *i.e.* the formula "Perhaps it is not," because it does not affirm in in regard to anything that it is really so. It is the same also in regard to the others.

194

195

CHAPTER XXII.

[Greek: epoche] *or the Suspension of Judgment.*

When I say that I suspend my judgment, I mean that I cannot say which of those things presented should be believed, and which should not be believed, showing that things appear equal to me in respect to trustworthiness and untrustworthiness. Now we do not affirm that they are equal, but we state what appears to us in regard to them at the time when they present themselves

196

to us. [Greek: epoche] means the holding back of the opinion, so as neither to affirm nor deny anything because of the equality of the things in question.

CHAPTER XXIII.

The Formula "I determine Nothing."

In regard to the formula "I determine nothing," we say the following: By "determine" we mean, not simply to speak, but to give assent to an affirmation with regard to some unknown thing. For it will soon be found that the Sceptic determines nothing, not even the formula "I determine nothing," for this formula is not a dogmatic opinion, that is an assent to something unknown, but an expression declaring what our condition of mind is. When, for example, the Sceptic says, "I determine nothing," he means this: "According to my present feeling I can assert or deny nothing dogmatically regarding the things under investigation," and in saying this he expresses what appears to him in reference to the things under discussion. He does not express himself positively, but he states what he feels.

197

CHAPTER XXIV.

The Formula "Every thing is Undetermined."

The expression "Indetermination" furthermore shows a state of mind in which we neither deny nor affirm positively anything regarding things that are investigated in a dogmatic way, that is the things that are unknown. When then the Sceptic says "Every thing is undetermined," he uses "is undetermined," in the sense of "it appears undetermined to him." The words "every thing" do not mean all existences, but those that he has examined of the unknown things that are investigated by the Dogmatists. By "undetermined," he means that there is no preference in the things that are placed in opposition to each other, or that they simply conflict with each other in respect to trustworthiness or untrustworthiness. And as the one who says "I am walking" really means "It is I that am walking," so he who says "Every thing is undetermined" means at the same time, according to our teachings, "as far as I am concerned," or "as it appears to me," as if he were saying "As far as I have examined the things that are under investigation in a dogmatic manner, it appears to me that no one of them excels the one which conflicts with it in trustworthiness or untrustworthiness."

198

199

CHAPTER XXV.

The Formula "Every thing is Incomprehensible."

We treat the formula "Every thing is incomprehensible" in 200
the same way. For "every thing" we interpret in the same way as
above, and we supply the words "to me" so that what we say is
this: "As far as I have inspected the unknown things which are
dogmatically examined, it appears to me that every thing is
incomprehensible." This is not, however, to affirm that the
things which are examined by the Dogmatists are of such a nature
as to be necessarily incomprehensible, but one expresses his own
feeling in saying "I see that I have not thus far comprehended
any of those things because of the equilibrium of the things
that are placed in opposition to each other." Whence it seems to
me that every thing that has been brought forward to dispute our
formulae has fallen wide of the mark.

CHAPTER XXVI.

The Formulae "I do not comprehend" and "I do not understand."

The formulae "I do not comprehend" and "I do not understand"   201
show a condition of mind in which the Sceptic stands aloof for
the present from asserting or denying anything in regard to the

unknown things under investigation, as is evident from what we said before about the other formulae.

CHAPTER XXVII.

The Formula "To place an equal Statement in opposition to every Statement."

Furthermore, when we say "Every statement may have an equal statement placed in opposition to it," by "every," we mean all the statements that we have examined; we do not use the word "statement" simply, but for a statement which seeks to prove something dogmatically about things that are unknown, and not at all one that shows a process of reasoning from premises and conclusions, but something which is put together in any sort of way. We use the word "equal" in reference to trustworthiness or untrustworthiness. "Is placed in opposition" we use instead of the common expression "to conflict with," and we supply "as it appears to me." When therefore one says, "It seems to me that every statement which I have examined, which proves something dogmatically, may have another statement placed in opposition to it which also proves something dogmatically, and which is equal to it in trustworthiness and untrustworthiness," this is not asserted dogmatically, but is an expression of human feeling as it appears to the one who feels it. Some Sceptics express the formula as follows: "Every statement should have an equal one placed in opposition to it," demanding it authoritatively thus: "Let us place in opposition to every statement that proves something dogmatically another conflicting 202 203 204 statement which also seeks to prove something dogmatically, and is equal to it in trustworthiness and untrustworthiness." Naturally this is directed to the Sceptics, but the infinitive should be used instead of the imperative, that is, "to oppose" instead of "let us oppose." This formula is recommended to the Sceptic, lest he should be deceived by the Dogmatists and give up his investigations, and rashly fail of the [Greek: ataraxia] which is thought to accompany [Greek: epoche] in regard to everything, as we have explained above.

CHAPTER XXVIII.

General Observations on the Formulae of the Sceptics.

We have treated of a sufficient number of these formulae for an outline, especially since what we have said about those mentioned applies also to others that we have omitted. In regard to all the Sceptical formulae, it must be understood in advance that we do not affirm them to be absolutely true, because we say that they can even refute themselves, since they are themselves included in those things to which they refer, just as cathartic medicines not only purge the body of humors, but carry off themselves with the humors. We say then that we use these formulae, not as literally making known the things for which they are used, but loosely, and if one wishes, inaccurately. It is not fitting for the Sceptic to dispute about words, especially as it contributes to our purpose to say that these formulae have no absolute meaning; their meaning is a relative one, that is, relative to the Sceptics. Besides, it is to be remembered that we do not say them about all things in general, but about the unknown, and things that are dogmatically investigated, and that we say what appears to us, and that we do not express ourselves decidedly about the nature of external objects. By this means I think that every sophism brought against the Sceptical formulae can be overturned. We have now shown the character of Scepticism by examining its idea, its parts, its criterion and aim, and also the Tropes of [Greek: epoche], and by treating of the Sceptical formulae. We think it therefore appropriate to enter briefly into the distinction between Scepticism and the nearly related schools of philosophy in order to more clearly understand the Sceptical School. We will begin with the philosophy of Heraclitus.

209

CHAPTER XXIX.

In what does the Sceptical School differ from the Philosophy of Heraclitus?

Now that this school differs from ours is evident, for Heraclitus expresses himself about many unknown things dogmatically, which we do not, as has been said. Aenesidemus and his followers said that the Sceptical School is the way to the philosophy of Heraclitus. They gave as a reason for this that the statement that contradictory predicates appear to be applicable to the same thing, leads the way to the statement that contradictory predicates are in reality applicable to the same thing; and as the Sceptics say that contradictory predicates appear to be applicable to the same thing, the

210

Heraclitans proceed from this to the doctrine that such predicates are in reality applicable. We reply to this that the statement that contradictory predicates appear to be applicable to the same thing is not a dogma of the Sceptics, but is a fact that presents itself not only to the Sceptics, but to other philosophers, and to all men. No one, for instance, would venture to say that honey does not taste sweet to those in health, and bitter to those who have the jaundice, so that the Heraclitans start from a preconception common to all men, as do we also, and perhaps the other schools of philosophy likewise. If, however, they had attributed the origin of the statement that contradictory predicates are present in the same thing to any of the Sceptical teachings, as, for example, to the formula "Every thing is incomprehensible," or "I determine nothing," or any of the other similar ones, it may be that which they say would follow; but since they start from that which is a common experience, not only to us, but to other philosophers, and in life, why should one say that our school is a path to the philosophy of Heraclitus more than any of the other schools of philosophy, or than life itself, as we all make use of the same subject matter? On the other hand, the Sceptical School may not only fail to help towards the knowledge of the philosophy of Heraclitus, but may even hinder it! For the Sceptic attacks all the dogmas of Heraclitus as having been rashly given, and opposes on the one hand the doctrine of conflagration, and on the other, the doctrine that contradictory predicates in reality apply to the same thing, and in regard to every dogma of Heraclitus he scorns his dogmatic rashness, and then, in the manner that I have before referred to, adduces the formulae "I do not understand" and "I determine nothing," which conflict with the Heraclitan doctrines. It is absurd to say that this conflicting school is a path to the very sect with which it conflicts. It is then absurd to say that the Sceptical School is

211

212

a path to the philosophy of Heraclitus.

CHAPTER XXX.

In what does the Sceptical School differ from the Philosophy of Democritus?

The philosophy of Democritus is also said to have community 213 with Scepticism, because it seems to use the same matter that we do. For, from the fact that honey seems sweet to some and bitter to others, Democritus reasons, it is said, that honey is neither sweet nor bitter, and therefore he accords with the formula "No more," which is a formula of the Sceptics. But the Sceptics and the Democritans use the formula "No more" differently from each other, for they emphasise the negation in the expression, but we, the not knowing whether both of the phenomena exist or neither one, and so we differ in this respect. The distinction, however, becomes most evident when Democritus says that 214 atoms and empty space are real, for by real he means existing in reality. Now, although he begins with the anomaly in phenomena, yet, since he says that atoms and empty space really exist, it is superfluous, I think, even to say that he differs from us.

CHAPTER XXXI.

In what does Scepticism differ from the Cyrenaic Philosophy?

Some say that the Cyrenaic School is the same as the Sceptical, because that school also claims to comprehend only conditions of mind. It differs, however, from it, because, while the former makes pleasure and the gentle motion of the flesh its aim, we make [Greek: ataraxia] ours, and this is opposed to the aim of their school. For whether pleasure is present or not, confusion awaits him who maintains that pleasure is an aim, as I have shown in what I said about the aim. And then, in addition, we suspend our judgment as far as the reasoning with regard to external objects is concerned, but the Cyrenaics pronounce the nature of these inscrutable.

215

CHAPTER XXXII.

In what does Scepticism differ from the Philosophy of Protagoras?

Protagoras makes man the measure of all things, of things that are that they are, and things that are not that they are not, meaning by measure, criterion, and by things, events, that is to say really, man is the criterion for all events, of things that are that they are, and of things that are not that they are

216

not. And for that reason he accepts only the phenomena that
appear to each man, and thus he introduces relation. Therefore   217
he seems to have community with the Pyrrhoneans. He differs,
however, from them, and we shall see the difference after we
have somewhat explained how things seemed to Protagoras. He
says, for example, that matter is fluid, and as it flows,
additions are constantly made in the place of that which is
carried away; the perceptions also are arranged anew and
changed, according to the age and according to other conditions
of the body. He says also, that the reasons of all phenomena 218
are present in matter, so that matter can be all that it appears
to be to all men as far as its power is concerned. Men, however,
apprehend differently at different times, according to the
different conditions that they are in; for he that is in a
natural condition will apprehend those qualities in matter that
can appear to those who are in a natural condition, while on   219
the contrary, those who are in an unnatural condition will
apprehend those qualities that can appear to the abnormal.
Furthermore, the same reasoning would hold true in regard to
differences in age, to sleeping and waking, and each of the
other different conditions. Therefore man becomes the criterion
of things that are, for all things that appear to men exist for
men, and those things that do not appear to any one among men do
not exist. We see that he dogmatises in saying that matter is
fluid, and also in saying that the reasons for all phenomena
have their foundation in matter, while these things are unknown,
and to us are things regarding which we suspend our judgment.

CHAPTER XXXIII.

In what does Scepticism differ from the Academic Philosophy?

Some say further that the Academic philosophy is the same as Scepticism, therefore it seems appropriate to me to treat of that also. There have been, as the most say, three Academies--the most ancient one, that of Plato and his followers; the second and middle one, that of Arcesilaus and his followers, Arcesilaus being the pupil of Polemo; the third and new Academy, that of Carneades and Clitomachus and their followers; some add also a fourth, that of Philo and Charmides, and their followers; and some count even a fifth, that of Antiochus and his followers. Beginning then from the old Academy, let us consider the difference between the schools of philosophy mentioned. Now some have said that Plato was a Dogmatic, others that he was a Sceptic, and others that he was in some things a Sceptic and in some things a Dogmatic. For in the fencing dialogues, where Socrates is introduced as either making sport of someone or contending against the Sophists, Plato has, they say, a fencing and sceptical character, but he is dogmatic when he expresses himself seriously, either through Socrates or Timaeus or any such person. In regard to those who say that he is a Dogmatic, or a Dogmatic in some things and a Sceptic in others, it would be superfluous, it seems to me, to speak now, for they themselves grant that he is different from us. The question as to whether he was really a Sceptic or not we treat more fully in the Memoranda, but here we state briefly that according to Menodotus and Aenesidemus (for these

220

221

222

especially defended this position) Plato dogmatises when he expresses himself regarding ideas, and regarding the existence of Providence, and when he states that the virtuous life is more to be chosen than the one of vice. If he assents to these things as true, he dogmatises; or even if he accepts them as more probable than otherwise he departs from the sceptical character, since he gives a preference to one thing above another in trustworthiness or untrustworthiness; for how foreign this is to us is evident from what we have said before. Even if when he performs mental gymnastics, as they say, he expresses some things sceptically, he is not because of this a Sceptic. For he who dogmatises about one thing, or, in short, gives preference to one mental image over another in trustworthiness or untrustworthiness in respect to anything that is unknown, is a Dogmatic in character, as Timon shows by what he said of Xenophanes. For after having praised Xenophanes in many things, and even after having dedicated his Satires to him, he made him mourn and say-- 223

224

"Would that I also might gain that mind profound,
Able to look both ways. In a treacherous path have I been decoyed,
And still in old age am with all wisdom unwed.
For wherever I turned my view
All things were resolved into unity; all things, alway
From all sources drawn, were merged into nature the same."

Timon calls him somewhat, but not entirely, free from vanity, when he said--

"Xenophanes somewhat free from vanity, mocker of
  Homeric deceit,
  Far from men he conceived a god, on all sides equal,

Above pain, a being spiritualised, or intellect."

In saying that he was somewhat free from vanity, he meant that he was in some things free from vanity. He called him a mocker of the Homeric deceit because he had scoffed at the deceit in Homer. Xenophanes also dogmatised, contrary to the assumptions 225 of other men, that all things are one, and that God is grown together with all things, that He is spherical, insensible, unchangeable, and reasonable, whence the difference of Xenophanes from us is easily proved. In short, from what has been said, it is evident that although Plato expresses doubt about some things, so long as he has expressed himself in certain places in regard to the existence of unknown things, or as preferring some things to others in trustworthiness, he cannot be, it seems to me, a Sceptic. Those of the New Academy, although they say that all things are incomprehensible, 226 differ from the Sceptics, perhaps even in saying that all things are incomprehensible (for they assert decidedly in regard to this, but the Sceptic thinks it possible that some things may be comprehended), but they differ evidently still further from us in their judgment of good and evil. For the Academicians say that there is such a thing as good and evil, not as we say it, but more with the conviction that that which they call good exists than that it does not; and likewise in regard to the evil, while we do not say anything is good or evil with the conviction that it is probably so, but we live our lives in an unprejudiced way in order not to be inactive. Moreover, we say that our ideas are equal to each other in trustworthiness 227 and untrustworthiness, as far as their nature goes, while they say that some are probable and others improbable. They make a difference also between the improbable ones, for they believe that some of them are only probable, others probable and undisputed, still others probable, undisputed, and tested. As for example, when a coiled rope is lying in a somewhat dark room, he who comes in suddenly gets only a probable idea of it, and thinks that it is a serpent; but it appears to be a rope 228 to him who has looked carefully around, and found out that it does not move, and that it is of such a color, and so on, according to an idea which is probable and undisputed. The tested idea is like this: It is said that Hercules led Alcestis after she was dead back again from Hades and showed her to Admetus, and he received an idea that was probable and undisputed regarding Alcestis. As, however, he knew that she was dead, his mind drew back from belief and inclined to disbelief. Now those belonging to the New Academy prefer the idea which 229 is probable and undisputed to the simply probable one. To both of these, however, they prefer that which is probable, undisputed, and tested. If, however, both those of the Academy and the Sceptics say that they believe certain things, there is an evident difference between the two schools of philosophy even in this; for "to believe" is used in a different sense, 230 meaning, on the one hand, not to resist, but simply to accept without strong inclination and approval, as the child is said to believe the teacher; on the other hand, "to believe" is used to signify assenting to something with choice, and, as it were, with the sympathy that accompanies strong will, as the prodigal follows the one who chooses to live a luxurious life. Therefore, since Carneades, Clitomachus, and their followers say that they are strongly inclined to believe that a thing is probable, and we simply allow that it may be so without assent, we differ 231 from them, I think, in this way. We differ from the New Academy likewise in things concerning the aim; for while the men who say that they govern themselves according to that School avail themselves of the idea of the probable in life, we live according to the laws and customs, and our natural feelings, in an unprejudiced way. We could say more regarding the distinction between the two schools if we did not aim at brevity. Nevertheless, Arcesilaus, who as we said was the leader and chief of the Middle Academy, seems to me to have very much in common with the Pyrrhonean teachings, so that his school and ours are almost one. For neither does one find that he expressed an opinion about the existence or non-existence of anything, nor does he prefer one thing to another as regards trustworthiness or untrustworthiness; he suspends his judgment regarding all things, and the aim of his philosophy is [Greek: epoche], which is accompanied by [Greek: ataraxia], and this agrees with what we have said. But he calls the particular instances of [Greek: epoche] ***bona***, and the particular instances of assent ***mala***. The difference is that we say these things according to what appears to us, and not affirmatively, while he says them as if speaking of realities, that is, he says that [Greek: epoche] is in itself good, and assent an evil. If we are to believe also the things that are said about him, he appeared at first sight to be a Pyrrhonean, but he was in truth a Dogmatic, for he used to test his companions by the method of doubt to see whether they were gifted enough to take in Plato's dogmas, so that he appeared to be a Sceptic, but at the same time he communicated the doctrines of Plato to those of his companions who were gifted. Hence Ariston also said about him--

"Plato in front, Pyrrhon behind, Diodorus in the middle,"

because he availed himself of the dialectic of Diodorus, but was wholly a Platonist. Now Philo and his followers say that as far as the Stoic criterion is concerned, that is to say the [Greek: phantasia kataleptike], things are incomprehensible, but as far as the nature of things is concerned, they are comprehensible. Antiochus, however, transferred the Stoa to the Academy, so that it was even said of him that he taught the

Stoic philosophy in the Academy, because he tried to show that the Stoic doctrines are found in Plato. The difference, therefore, between the Sceptical School and the Fourth and Fifth Academy is evident.

CHAPTER XXXIV.

Is Empiricism in Medicine the same as Scepticism?

Some say that the medical sect called Empiricism is the same as Scepticism. Yet the fact must be recognised, that even if Empiricism does maintain the impossibility of knowledge, it is neither Scepticism itself, nor would it suit the Sceptic to take that sect upon himself. He could rather, it seems to me, belong to the so-called Methodic School. For this alone, of all the medical sects, does not seem to proceed rashly in regard to unknown things, and does not presume to say whether they are comprehensible or not, but is guided by phenomena, and receives from them the same help which they seem to give to the Sceptical system. For we have said in what has gone before, that the every-day life which the Sceptic lives is of four parts, depending on the guidance of nature, on the necessity of the feelings, on the traditions of laws and customs, and on the teaching of the arts. Now as by necessity of the feelings the Sceptic is led by thirst to drink, and by hunger to food, and to supply similar needs in the same way, so also the physician of the Methodic School is led by the feelings to find suitable remedies; in constipation he produces a relaxation, as one takes refuge in the sun from the shrinking on account of intense cold; he is led by a flux to the stopping of it, as those in a hot bath who are dripping from a profuse perspiration and are relaxed, hasten to check it by going into the cold air. Moreover, it is evident that the Methodic physician forces those things which are of a foreign nature to adapt themselves to their own nature, as even the dog tries to get a sharp stick out that is thrust into him. In order, however, that I should not overstep the outline character of this work by discussing details, I think that all the things that the Methodics have thus said can be classified as referring to the necessity of the feelings that are natural or those that are unnatural. Besides this, it is common to both schools to have no dogmas, and to use words loosely. For as the Sceptic uses the formula "I determine nothing," and "I understand nothing," as we said above, so the Methodic also uses the expressions "Community," and "To go through," and other similar ones without over much care. In a similar way he uses the word "Indication" undogmatically, meaning that the symptoms of the patient either natural or unnatural, indicate the remedies that would be suitable, as we said in speaking of thirst, hunger, and other things. It will thus be seen that the Methodic School of medicine has a certain relationship to Scepticism which is closer than that of the other medical sects, speaking comparatively if not absolutely from these and similar tokens. Having said so much in reference to the schools that seem to closely resemble Scepticism, we conclude the general consideration of Scepticism and the First Book of the Sketches.

www.bookjungle.com *email: sales@bookjungle.com fax: 630-214-0564 mail: Book Jungle PO Box 2226 Champaign, IL 61825*

The Codes Of Hammurabi And Moses
W. W. Davies

QTY

The discovery of the Hammurabi Code is one of the greatest achievements of archaeology, and is of paramount interest, not only to the student of the Bible, but also to all those interested in ancient history...

Religion   ISBN: *1-59462-338-4*   Pages:132
MSRP $12.95

The Theory of Moral Sentiments
Adam Smith

QTY

This work from 1749. contains original theories of conscience amd moral judgment and it is the foundation for systemof morals.

Philosophy   ISBN: *1-59462-777-0*   Pages:536
MSRP $19.95

Jessica's First Prayer
Hesba Stretton

QTY

In a screened and secluded corner of one of the many railway-bridges which span the streets of London there could be seen a few years ago, from five o'clock every morning until half past eight, a tidily set-out coffee-stall, consisting of a trestle and board, upon which stood two large tin cans, with a small fire of charcoal burning under each so as to keep the coffee boiling during the early hours of the morning when the work-people were thronging into the city on their way to their daily toil...

Childrens   ISBN: *1-59462-373-2*   Pages:84
MSRP $9.95

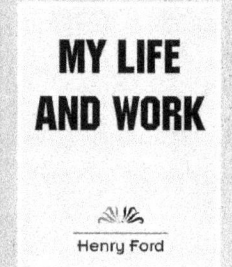

My Life and Work
Henry Ford

QTY

Henry Ford revolutionized the world with his implementation of mass production for the Model T automobile. Gain valuable business insight into his life and work with his own auto-biography... "We have only started on our development of our country we have not as yet, with all our talk of wonderful progress, done more than scratch the surface. The progress has been wonderful enough but..."

Biographies/   ISBN: *1-59462-198-5*   Pages:300
MSRP $21.95

www.bookjungle.com email: sales@bookjungle.com fax: 630-214-0564 mail: Book Jungle PO Box 2226 Champaign, IL 61825

The Art of Cross-Examination
Francis Wellman

QTY

I presume it is the experience of every author, after his first book is published upon an important subject, to be almost overwhelmed with a wealth of ideas and illustrations which could readily have been included in his book, and which to his own mind, at least, seem to make a second edition inevitable. Such certainly was the case with me; and when the first edition had reached its sixth impression in five months, I rejoiced to learn that it seemed to my publishers that the book had met with a sufficiently favorable reception to justify a second and considerably enlarged edition. ..

Reference   ISBN: *1-59462-647-2*   Pages:412   MSRP *$19.95*

On the Duty of Civil Disobedience
Henry David Thoreau

QTY

Thoreau wrote his famous essay, On the Duty of Civil Disobedience, as a protest against an unjust but popular war and the immoral but popular institution of slave-owning. He did more than write—he declined to pay his taxes, and was hauled off to gaol in consequence. Who can say how much this refusal of his hastened the end of the war and of slavery ?

Law   ISBN: *1-59462-747-9*   Pages:48   MSRP *$7.45*

Dream Psychology Psychoanalysis for Beginners
Sigmund Freud

QTY

Sigmund Freud, born Sigismund Schlomo Freud (May 6, 1856 - September 23, 1939), was a Jewish-Austrian neurologist and psychiatrist who co-founded the psychoanalytic school of psychology. Freud is best known for his theories of the unconscious mind, especially involving the mechanism of repression; his redefinition of sexual desire as mobile and directed towards a wide variety of objects; and his therapeutic techniques, especially his understanding of transference in the therapeutic relationship and the presumed value of dreams as sources of insight into unconscious desires.

Psychology   ISBN: *1-59462-905-6*   Pages:196   MSRP *$15.45*

The Miracle of Right Thought
Orison Swett Marden

QTY

Believe with all of your heart that you will do what you were made to do. When the mind has once formed the habit of holding cheerful, happy, prosperous pictures, it will not be easy to form the opposite habit. It does not matter how improbable or how far away this realization may see, or how dark the prospects may be, if we visualize them as best we can, as vividly as possible, hold tenaciously to them and vigorously struggle to attain them, they will gradually become actualized, realized in the life. But a desire, a longing without endeavor, a yearning abandoned or held indifferently will vanish without realization.

Self Help   ISBN: *1-59462-644-8*   Pages:360   MSRP *$25.45*

www.bookjungle.com email: sales@bookjungle.com fax: 630-214-0564 mail: Book Jungle PO Box 2226 Champaign, IL 61825

QTY

	Title	ISBN	Price
☐	**The Rosicrucian Cosmo-Conception Mystic Christianity** by *Max Heindel*	ISBN: 1-59462-188-8	$38.95
	The Rosicrucian Cosmo-conception is not dogmatic, neither does it appeal to any other authority than the reason of the student. It is: not controversial, but is: sent forth in the, hope that it may help to clear...		New Age/Religion Pages 646
☐	**Abandonment To Divine Providence** by *Jean-Pierre de Caussade*	ISBN: 1-59462-228-0	$25.95
	"The Rev. Jean Pierre de Caussade was one of the most remarkable spiritual writers of the Society of Jesus in France in the 18th Century. His death took place at Toulouse in 1751. His works have gone through many editions and have been republished...		Inspirational/Religion Pages 400
☐	**Mental Chemistry** by *Charles Haanel*	ISBN: 1-59462-192-6	$23.95
	Mental Chemistry allows the change of material conditions by combining and appropriately utilizing the power of the mind. Much like applied chemistry creates something new and unique out of careful combinations of chemicals the mastery of mental chemistry...		New Age Pages 354
☐	**The Letters of Robert Browning and Elizabeth Barret Barrett 1845-1846 vol II** by *Robert Browning and Elizabeth Barrett*	ISBN: 1-59462-193-4	$35.95
			Biographies Pages 596
☐	**Gleanings In Genesis (volume I)** by *Arthur W. Pink*	ISBN: 1-59462-130-6	$27.45
	Appropriately has Genesis been termed "the seed plot of the Bible" for in it we have, in germ form, almost all of the great doctrines which are afterwards fully developed in the books of Scripture which follow...		Religion/Inspirational Pages 420
☐	**The Master Key** by *L. W. de Laurence*	ISBN: 1-59462-001-6	$30.95
	In no branch of human knowledge has there been a more lively increase of the spirit of research during the past few years than in the study of Psychology, Concentration and Mental Discipline. The requests for authentic lessons in Thought Control, Mental Discipline and...		New Age/Business Pages 422
☐	**The Lesser Key Of Solomon Goetia** by *L. W. de Laurence*	ISBN: 1-59462-092-X	$9.95
	This translation of the first book of the "Lemegton" which is now for the first time made accessible to students of Talismanic Magic was done, after careful collation and edition, from numerous Ancient Manuscripts in Hebrew, Latin, and French...		New Age/Occult Pages 92
☐	**Rubaiyat Of Omar Khayyam** by *Edward Fitzgerald*	ISBN: 1-59462-332-5	$13.95
	Edward Fitzgerald, whom the world has already learned, in spite of his own efforts to remain within the shadow of anonymity, to look upon as one of the rarest poets of the century, was born at Bredfield, in Suffolk, on the 31st of March, 1809. He was the third son of John Purcell...		Music Pages 172
☐	**Ancient Law** by *Henry Maine*	ISBN: 1-59462-128-4	$29.95
	The chief object of the following pages is to indicate some of the earliest ideas of mankind, as they are reflected in Ancient Law, and to point out the relation of those ideas to modern thought.		Religion/History Pages 452
☐	**Far-Away Stories** by *William J. Locke*	ISBN: 1-59462-129-2	$19.45
	"Good wine needs no bush, but a collection of mixed vintages does. And this book is just such a collection. Some of the stories I do not want to remain buried for ever in the museum files of dead magazine-numbers an author's not unpardonable vanity..."		Fiction Pages 272
☐	**Life of David Crockett** by *David Crockett*	ISBN: 1-59462-250-7	$27.45
	"Colonel David Crockett was one of the most remarkable men of the times in which he lived. Born in humble life, but gifted with a strong will, an indomitable courage, and unremitting perseverance...		Biographies/New Age Pages 424
☐	**Lip-Reading** by *Edward Nitchie*	ISBN: 1-59462-206-X	$25.95
	Edward B. Nitchie, founder of the New York School for the Hard of Hearing, now the Nitchie School of Lip-Reading, Inc, wrote "LIP-READING Principles and Practice". The development and perfecting of this meritorious work on lip-reading was an undertaking...		How-to Pages 400
☐	**A Handbook of Suggestive Therapeutics, Applied Hypnotism, Psychic Science** by *Henry Munro*	ISBN: 1-59462-214-0	$24.95
			Health/New Age/Health/Self-help Pages 376
☐	**A Doll's House: and Two Other Plays** by *Henrik Ibsen*	ISBN: 1-59462-112-8	$19.95
	Henrik Ibsen created this classic when in revolutionary 1848 Rome. Introducing some striking concepts in playwriting for the realist genre, this play has been studied the world over.		Fiction/Classics/Plays 308
☐	**The Light of Asia** by *sir Edwin Arnold*	ISBN: 1-59462-204-3	$13.95
	In this poetic masterpiece, Edwin Arnold describes the life and teachings of Buddha. The man who was to become known as Buddha to the world was born as Prince Gautama of India but he rejected the worldly riches and abandoned the reigns of power when...		Religion/History/Biographies Pages 170
☐	**The Complete Works of Guy de Maupassant** by *Guy de Maupassant*	ISBN: 1-59462-157-8	$16.95
	"For days and days, nights and nights, I had dreamed of that first kiss which was to consecrate our engagement, and I knew not on what spot I should put my lips..."		Fiction/Classics Pages 240
☐	**The Art of Cross-Examination** by *Francis L. Wellman*	ISBN: 1-59462-309-0	$26.95
	Written by a renowned trial lawyer, Wellman imparts his experience and uses case studies to explain how to use psychology to extract desired information through questioning.		How-to/Science/Reference Pages 408
☐	**Answered or Unanswered?** by *Louisa Vaughan*	ISBN: 1-59462-248-5	$10.95
	Miracles of Faith in China		Religion Pages 112
☐	**The Edinburgh Lectures on Mental Science (1909)** by *Thomas*	ISBN: 1-59462-008-3	$11.95
	This book contains the substance of a course of lectures recently given by the writer in the Queen Street Hall, Edinburgh. Its purpose is to indicate the Natural Principles governing the relation between Mental Action and Material Conditions...		New Age/Psychology Pages 148
☐	**Ayesha** by *H. Rider Haggard*	ISBN: 1-59462-301-5	$24.95
	Verily and indeed it is the unexpected that happens! Probably if there was one person upon the earth from whom the Editor of this, and of a certain previous history, did not expect to hear again...		Classics Pages 380
☐	**Ayala's Angel** by *Anthony Trollope*	ISBN: 1-59462-352-X	$29.95
	The two girls were both pretty, but Lucy who was twenty-one who supposed to be simple and comparatively unattractive, whereas Ayala was credited, as her Bombwhat romantic name might show, with poetic charm and a taste for romance. Ayala when her father died was nineteen...		Fiction Pages 484
☐	**The American Commonwealth** by *James Bryce*	ISBN: 1-59462-286-8	$34.45
	An interpretation of American democratic political theory. It examines political mechanics and society from the perspective of Scotsman James Bryce		Politics Pages 572
☐	**Stories of the Pilgrims** by *Margaret P. Pumphrey*	ISBN: 1-59462-116-0	$17.95
	This book explores pilgrims religious oppression in England as well as their escape to Holland and eventual crossing to America on the Mayflower, and their early days in New England...		History Pages 268

www.bookjungle.com email: sales@bookjungle.com fax: 630-214-0564 mail: Book Jungle PO Box 2226 Champaign, IL 61825

QTY

The Fasting Cure *by Sinclair Upton* ISBN: *1-59462-222-1* **$13.95**
In the Cosmopolitan Magazine for May, 1910, and in the Contemporary Review (London) for April, 1910, I published an article dealing with my experiences in fasting. I have written a great many magazine articles, but never one which attracted so much attention... New Age/Self Help/Health Pages 164

Hebrew Astrology *by Sepharial* ISBN: *1-59462-308-0* **$13.45**
In these days of advanced thinking it is a matter of common observation that we have left many of the old landmarks behind and that we are now pressing forward to greater heights and to a wider horizon than that which represented the mind-content of our progenitors... Astrology Pages 144

Thought Vibration or The Law of Attraction in the Thought World ISBN: *1-59462-127-6* **$12.95**
by William Walker Atkinson Psychology/Religion Pages 144

Optimism *by Helen Keller* ISBN: *1-59462-108-X* **$15.95**
Helen Keller was blind, deaf, and mute since 19 months old, yet famously learned how to overcome these handicaps, communicate with the world, and spread her lectures promoting optimism. An inspiring read for everyone... Biographies/Inspirational Pages 84

Sara Crewe *by Frances Burnett* ISBN: *1-59462-360-0* **$9.45**
In the first place, Miss Minchin lived in London. Her home was a large, dull, tall one, in a large, dull square, where all the houses were alike, and all the sparrows were alike, and where all the door-knockers made the same heavy sound... Childrens/Classic Pages 88

The Autobiography of Benjamin Franklin *by Benjamin Franklin* ISBN: *1-59462-135-7* **$24.95**
The Autobiography of Benjamin Franklin has probably been more extensively read than any other American historical work, and no other book of its kind has had such ups and downs of fortune. Franklin lived for many years in England, where he was agent... Biographies/History Pages 332

Name	
Email	
Telephone	
Address	
City, State ZIP	

☐ Credit Card   ☐ Check / Money Order

Credit Card Number	
Expiration Date	
Signature	

Please Mail to: Book Jungle
PO Box 2226
Champaign, IL 61825
or Fax to: 630-214-0564

ORDERING INFORMATION
web: *www.bookjungle.com*
email: *sales@bookjungle.com*
fax: *630-214-0564*
mail: *Book Jungle PO Box 2226 Champaign, IL 61825*
or PayPal *to sales@bookjungle.com*

Please contact us for bulk discounts

DIRECT-ORDER TERMS

**20% Discount if You Order
Two or More Books**
Free Domestic Shipping!
Accepted: Master Card, Visa,
Discover, American Express

www.ingramcontent.com/pod-product-compliance
Lightning Source LLC
Chambersburg PA
CBHW081231170426
43198CB00017B/2717